DeLayne Toews

D0864379

Double Take

Enjoy hunting for
treasures!
Tim Geddert

Double Take

New Meanings From Old Stories

By Timothy J. Geddert

Kindred Productions is the publishing arm for the Mennonite Brethren Churches. Kindred publishes, promotes and markets print and mixed media resources that help shape our Christian faith and discipleship from the Mennonite Brethren perspective.

Published simultaneously by Kindred Books, an imprint of Kindred Productions, Winnipeg, MB R3M 3Z6 and Kindred Productions, Hillsboro KS 67063.

Cover design and photography by Brad Thiessen
Illustration on page 112 by Jurgen Penner
Printed in Canada by Friesens

Library and Archives Canada Cataloguing in Publication

Geddert, Timothy J.
      Double take : new meanings from old stories / Timothy J. Geddert.

ISBN 978-1-894791-13-7

      1. Bible--Criticism, interpretation, etc. I. Title.

BS511.3.G44 2007   220.6   C2007-903121-8

International Standard Book Number: 978-1-894791-13-7

Table of Contents

Introduction

Hunting for Treasures
in Familiar Places

I remember it as though it were yesterday. Who wouldn't? After all, a genuine "Aha" experience is rare – and two of them in the same evening, even more rare. We were sitting in a circle. I was leading a Bible study in a small congregation. Well, it might be more accurate to say I was showing off how much I had learned about the Gospel of Mark in the first year of my doctoral studies.

At a crucial point of interpretation, Brad, a member of the youth group, made an interesting comment in response to what I had just said. He was sharing his insight, sparked by mine. For the next ten seconds, I was hardly present (except physically) with the Bible study group. It was as though my mind was filled with "click! click! YES! and click!" … filled with miscellaneous pieces of my far-from-finished-dissertation falling into place. And while part of my mind was quickly reconstructing a section of my dissertation, another part was saying: "Now, I've read dozens of scholarly books and hundreds of articles … but never did anyone point me to the insight, the obvious one, that Brad just articulated!"

Somehow I returned to leading the Bible study. But I went home having learned something terribly important about the book of Mark …and having learned something even more important about being open to new insights into the meaning of Scripture, even if they come from unexpected people in unexpected places.

This book contains insights that I've gained by reading scholarly literature, and by reading the texts of Scripture in the original languages and with technical exegetical tools. But it contains at least as many that were sparked because one of my students, or a member of a youth group, or a keen Bible student in a Sunday school class made the kind of comment that simply made my mind say, "What an insight! I may need to look at this text in a new way!"

––––––––––––

The two greatest enemies of Bible interpretation are:
1. Knowing too little, and
2. Knowing too much.
Ironically, these two dangers are almost identical.

Those who "know too little" are usually those who are sure that the plain meaning of Scripture (plain to them, anyway!) is the only meaning there is. Those who "know too little" are sure that the Bible always speaks clearly. Whatever cannot be seen clearly on the surface of the text is not there to be found. We don't dig deeper lest we be distracted from what the Bible clearly teaches. We don't ask about cultural and historical backgrounds because that will just lead us to "evade the plain meaning" of Scripture. And we neither learn the original languages nor consult those who do. After all, scholars can make a text mean almost anything (these people think), and they are, with few exceptions, not to be trusted.

Those who "know too much" have no need to learn more. They know the Bible. They have been taught it all their lives. They learned all the stories in Sunday school and the correct interpretation of all the difficult passages in Sunday morning sermons. They are convinced that there is an unbroken line of faithful and correct biblical interpretation that has withstood all the heresies of church history and been passed on faithfully through their own tradition and denomination. Every text means exactly what it has always meant. "If it is new it is not true and if it is true it is not new" (as I once heard a radio preacher insist).

People who know too little have few resources with which to learn more. Their minds cannot stretch. People who know too much have no motivation to learn more. Their minds are made up. Either way, Bible interpretation is either uninteresting or unimportant. After all, what is there to learn?

My greatest delight as a Bible teacher is to guide people safely out of range of both of those dangers, and then move with them toward that place where interpreting the Bible is a never-ending adventure. As tools are developed, curiosity is piqued, creativity is encouraged, and the guiding presence of God's Spirit and God's people are sensed, students

––––––––––––

"launch out into the deep" and let out their nets for a catch. Sometimes the good fish and bad fish still need to be separated afterward, but there is the excitement of discovery. The Bible becomes a living book. The Christian life becomes an adventure. Preaching and teaching become interesting and provocative and life-changing.

One day, Jesus sat in a boat and taught people crowded along the shore. Later, he retires with his disciples to a house to explain some of his earlier lessons and teach some new ones.

Suddenly, out of the blue, comes Jesus' question: "Have you understood all these things?" (cf. Matt. 13:51). The question is addressed to "disciples" (the word means "learner"). Jesus is doing a reality check: are they really learning? Is the teaching going over their heads? Or in one ear and out the other?

I don't know which answer Jesus expected, but the one he gets raises some questions in my mind: "Yes!" That's the answer they give. Now they might have answered:

"Well, we think we are getting most of it."
    or
"We think so, but could you go over that last part again, please?"
    or
"No, we can't keep up! This won't be on the exam, will it?"

Instead they say, "Yes!"
So how does Jesus respond? He might have said:

"Great! I'm proud of you; you are great students!"
    or
"I knew you were paying attention; you can take a break now."
    or
"Really? Well, we'll see when exam week arrives."

Instead he says this:
"Therefore every teacher of the law who has been instructed about the kingdom of heaven is like the owner of a house who brings out of his storeroom new treasures as well as old" (13:52).

What is he saying? Is he saying:

"Great! You deserve a prize! I'll go get a treasure for each of you."
    or
"Wonderful! Then you have already found all the hidden treasures."
    or
"Well, if the other parables were so easy, try this one?"

I think Jesus means something else. He refers to "scribes who have been trained." That's a graphic and surprising expression, for it literally means, "people who know it all but have now become learners again." In Jesus' day, scribes were experts in the Scriptures. The word "scribe" meant literally, "man of letters" (the religious scholars were all men in those days). They had mastered the "letter of the law." They understood the grammar of every sentence. But, according to Jesus, that in itself does not make someone fit for the Kingdom of Heaven. One must first undergo a transformation.

When Jesus speaks of "scribes who have been trained," he really means "re-trained," for the word means literally "having become disciples/learners." It's the same word Jesus uses when he commissioned his followers to "make disciples of all nations." According to Jesus, one does not qualify for membership in God's Kingdom by being a "scribe." The entrance requirement is being a "disciple." You don't get in by knowing-it-all, but by being a learner.

Now we see how Jesus' parable fits the situation at hand. Jesus' disciples (his learners) claim that they already understand everything. Is that what they think Jesus wants from them? Jesus knows that the biggest enemy of discipleship is thinking one knows everything. Instead of congratulating (or scolding) them, Jesus simply says, "Let me tell you how this works. True disciples never claim to understand everything. Disciples are learners, not know-it-alls. If you've turned into 'scribes,' the only thing left is to turn back into disciples!"

The goal of discipleship is to keep learning; we do not claim to understand everything. For learners, there is a storehouse of treasures waiting to be discovered. Some of the treasures are old – they've been discovered by millions throughout the ages. And some are new – other people have not discovered them, or at any rate, many have not. They are there to be found and treasured!

I am always saddened when I encounter people who come to the Scriptures with the attitude of a scribe – they already understand it all. They bring with them no sense of discovery or adventure; they have no expectation of discovering something new. Coming to Scriptures with a closed mind is almost as sad as leaving the Scriptures closed in the first place.

This book is about the adventure of learning new things in our study of the Bible. It is not so much a book of method as a book of examples. But from beginning to end, it's my aim to help readers reflect on what opens up the message of Scripture for the curious reader. And from beginning to end, I also aim to help readers discover that new insights are a wonderful blessing: sometimes they bring new truths to light that would otherwise remain hidden from us; sometimes they solve a puzzle in a text that has genuinely bothered us; sometimes they help us understand why our experiences do not match what we thought a text was teaching. Discovering new things in Scripture can rekindle our joy in searching for truth – both in Scripture and in its divine author. Sometimes it can unsettle our naïve conviction that we have it all figured out. If this last one doesn't seem like a blessing, it is! Have you ever noticed how much more interesting preachers and teachers are if they are learners themselves?

But some may ask, "Why is it important to keep searching the Scriptures? Haven't previous generations of Christians already figured out what each text means?" Indeed, they did the best with the tools and the convictions they had. We do the best with ours. And those who come after us will do the best they can with theirs. Isn't that what it means for God's Word to continue to challenge and inspire in every generation?

There are numerous passages in Scripture, indeed hundreds of them, where my present understanding coincides with the interpretations I learned in Sunday school, in youth group meetings, in Bible school and in countless sermons. This book contains samples of those other texts, where my thinking has changed along the way. If anyone reads this book as though it were really saying:

"Don't trust your Sunday school teachers!"
    or

"English translations are usually wrong."
> or

"One needs to know Greek to understand the Bible."
> or

"Scholars are always challenging traditional beliefs!"
> or

"What a know-it-all the author is!"

... they will have missed the whole point. My goals are very different. If this book accomplishes some of the following goals, I will be thrilled:

- to awaken in each reader a sense of adventure in studying the Bible (I hope each reader has at least a few "aha" experiences);
- to help readers recognize the importance of probing deeply and creatively, as well as using appropriate tools when interpreting Scripture (even a few simple word studies can make a world of difference!);
- to show readers that more is gained than lost when we are willing to allow some of our preconceived notions and inherited traditions to be questioned (I may be a bit unsettled occasionally, but what is that compared to losing my faith because a misunderstood "promise" was never fulfilled?);
- to bring into public discussion a number of "new interpretations" so that they can be discerned by the Christian community (you didn't think I considered my view to be the final word, I hope!);
- and finally, but not least important, to provide new glimpses of God and of God's way of working in our lives (and I know of no more effective way of keeping the joy of Bible study alive than that).

"How do you come up with new discoveries?" my students have sometimes asked me. My most important answer is that I desire to find them, and so I keep my eyes open for them everywhere: in books I read, in the inductive Bible studies I lead or practice myself, in the comments students make and in the papers they write, in discussions with people from other traditions than my own. And when I see glimpses of new ideas, I pursue them, and test them, and often discard them, but sometimes find they truly shed new light on the text at hand. Many of the new discoveries shared in this book were not originally sparked by technical scholarly writings, nor discovered because I was able to read the texts in their original languages. Many came because there was a group of eager Bible students who were sitting in a circle, reading the texts carefully and asking helpful and creative questions that led to new (and in my opinion sometimes valid and important) insights. Others did come by reading learned books, and yes, some by reading the text in Greek. But in each chapter, I have tried to explain my understanding in a way that is transparent enough for any serious Bible student to join in the dialogue, share in the discoveries, and help me distinguish between new treasures and "an interesting idea that just doesn't quite work." Do I personally believe that all the interpretations offered in the following pages are correct? Yes and no. Yes, they all represent my present opinion, and I have never yet met a person who did not consider their own opinions to be correct. But, no, I could never claim to be certain that these interpretations are the right ones for each text. It is precisely that kind of "I-know-I-am-right" attitude that keeps people from the kind of new discoveries this book encourages them to make.

So what are the following articles about?

- All are about Scripture interpretation (though none provides detailed technical discussions of exegetical methodology).
- All attempt to shed light on the meaning of one (occasionally more than one) biblical text.
- All are about the life of the Christian and the church, for many of these were created originally as part of my preparation for preaching and teaching.
- Many are about the right and wrong expectations we have of ourselves as Christians, and also of God. We often live frustrated lives, experiencing either guilt or disappointment because we do not experience what we thought the Bible led us to expect. And I'm sure sometimes our faith is too small or we have to learn to live with disappointment. But sometimes we simply need to go back to Scripture and honestly ask: "Does this text really say what I've always thought it did?"

Why are most of the chapters about New Testament texts? Definitely not because that is the only part of Scripture that contains treasures. It's just that I have spent more time hunting for treasures in the New Testament than in the Old. For the same reason there are more contributions from Mark than anywhere else. This surely implies that there are far more treasures waiting to be found, if only we will take the time to look!

What logic determines the order in which these interpretations are presented? After trying out many other options, I decided simply to follow the order the texts appear in the Bible, deviating from that order only where two chapters seemed like they should be arranged consecutively. Perhaps some will find in this book "new treasures as well as old." Others might quickly discern the need to "separate the good fish from the bad." I can only hope that most readers will catch a bit of the spirit of adventure that makes studying the Bible richly rewarding and often fun.

Finally, I'd like to pass along some thanks. First, to my students, who have often given me good feedback on my interpretations. Second, thank you to my teaching assistants who have helped me edit the various chapters. Kristin Fast helped edit quite a number, and contributed significantly to my interpretation of Luke 18:1-8. Ryan Schellenberg helped me edit most of the others. Thanks, Jurgen Penner, for the sketch on page 112. Last, thank you to Brad Thiessen for his encouragement to publish these interpretations and then for making it happen.

When I am Weak,
Then I am Strong!

Judges 6,7 and 2 Corinthians 4

Paul claimed, more than once, that it is in weakness that we experience God's strength. Yet often it is precisely because we are unaware that God's strength is available to us that we experience ourselves as weak – weak in faith, helpless to withstand temptation, unprepared for the challenges of the Christian life and of ministry.

Here we have something to learn from Gideon, a man who thought himself too weak to be of service to God, until he learned that sometimes it is the strong who do not really have what it takes to succeed. Gideon did not feel particularly honored when God called him and his tiny army to accomplish "Mission Impossible." Just as we sometimes do, Gideon responded to God's call by saying, "I'm too small! I'm too weak! You really expect me to accomplish that?"

Gideon lived during a very difficult time in Israel's history. Israel had been freed from Egypt and led into the Promised Land. They had defeated many enemies, but the land in which they had come to live was really not yet their possession.

Israel had to share this land with many of the nations and tribes who had lived there before their arrival. And the relationships between the Israelites and these other people were full of tension and conflict. In this context Israel was constantly tempted to worship the false gods of the surrounding nations.

In one of the darkest of these times, Midian was the powerful foreign oppressor. And that is when God called Gideon. His task would be to free Israel from Midian and bring the Israelites back to their God.

Gideon was neither a particularly great man, nor especially strong. He did not have a particularly strong faith, nor a great interest in hearing

God's voice or God's call. When God promised Gideon that with God's strength he would successfully carry out his mission, he didn't really believe it. More than once he demanded a sign that God was really there calling him to the task.

Let's remind ourselves of part of the story (Judges 6:12-17):

> When the angel of the LORD appeared to Gideon, he said, "The LORD is with you, mighty warrior."
>
> "But sir," Gideon replied, "if the LORD is with us, why has all this happened to us? Where are all his wonders that our fathers told us about when they said, 'Did not the LORD bring us up out of Egypt?' But now the LORD has abandoned us and put us into the hand of Midian."
>
> The LORD turned to him and said, "Go in the strength you have and save Israel out of Midian's hand. Am I not sending you?"
>
> "But Lord," Gideon asked, "how can I save Israel? My clan is the weakest in Manasseh, and I am the least in my family."
>
> The LORD answered, "I will be with you, and you will strike down all the Midianites together."
>
> Gideon replied, "If now I have found favor in your eyes, give me a sign that it is really you talking to me."

And so God gave Gideon a sign by sending fire down from heaven to burn his offering. But that wasn't enough. Gideon devised two more tests – fleeces, we call them today – demanding that God prove it was really a divine messenger calling Gideon. God acted to strengthen Gideon's weak faith.

God provided Gideon with the proof he needed that divine help would accompany the divine call on his life, and that he would be able to defeat Israel's enemy. There is a turning point in the story, when Gideon finally stops saying, "I am too weak; I am too small!"

Gideon gathers an army of about 32,000 soldiers. Finally he's ready to go into battle against Midian. *But now God is not ready to send him!* Gideon hasn't quite learned his lesson correctly. He has indeed learned that God was not impressed with his excuses: I'm too weak; I'm too small. Unfortunately, he now believes he is indeed strong enough and great enough. Gideon has jumped from an error on one side, to an equally dangerous one on the other.

God does not want Gideon to replace "I am too weak" with "I am strong enough." God wants Gideon to replace "*I* am too weak" with "*You* are strong enough." That is what Gideon does not yet understand. He thinks God has been trying to teach him that the Israelite army under his leadership will indeed be strong enough to destroy the Midianites. But Gideon is not strong enough. Neither is Israel's army. Were they to act in their own power, they would go down to certain defeat.

No, Gideon, God does not want to convince you that you and your nation are strong enough! God wants you to learn that you are not too weak; you are exactly as weak as God wants you to be. Your weakness combined with your faith in God will release all the power necessary to defeat the Midianites. God will win the victory *despite* your weakness, indeed *through* your weakness.

And so, as Gideon and his 32,000 soldiers begin their military maneuvers, God suddenly calls, "*Halt!* Gideon, you are not ready." This is how God puts it (Judges 7:2a, NRSV):

> The troops with you are too many for me to give the Midianites into their hand.

To paraphrase, "Gideon, at first you thought that you were too weak. You weren't! You were exactly as weak as I wanted you to be. That is why I called you! With the precise amount of strength and weakness that you have, I can win the victory through you. If you want to win in your own strength, then you are still far too weak! And if you want to win in my strength, then you have now become far too strong."

What kind of strange military strategy is God working with? Too strong to win? You have to become weaker? Yes, that is God's military strategy. In fact, it's God's strategy in many situations.

And so God explains to Gideon why the army he has gathered is now too big (Judges 7:2b, NRSV):

> The troops with you are too many for me to give the Midianites into their hand. Israel would only take the credit away from me, saying, "My own hand has delivered me."

Gideon must reduce the size of his army. Only if the victory comes through a small army will it be clear to everyone that God is the one who gives the victory. Only those who know that they are weak can put the power of God on display. All others give the impression they did it in their own strength.

And so Gideon sends 22,000 soldiers home. Then he sends almost another 10,000 home. In the end, only a small army of three hundred remains, ready to go out and win the battle in the power of the Lord. Now the army is small enough. Now nobody will ever think human strength has won the battle. Now it will be clear to everyone that the victory belongs to the Lord.

And then, just to make sure that the lesson is well learned, God sends Gideon and his little army into battle with the most unusual weapons you can imagine: trumpets, empty clay pots and torches: no swords, no canons, no missiles.

The torches will be hidden in the clay pots. At the given signal the trumpets will be blown, the clay pots will be broken and the torches will be held high!

Gideon's army is naïve enough, *believing* enough, *recklessly obedient* enough, to do what God says. And God gives them the victory. They don't need any swords. As the lights suddenly shine into the darkness, the Midianites start using their own swords against each other.

Three hundred men win the victory. No, that would be the wrong way to describe what happens. God wins the victory because there were three hundred men willing to recognize their own weakness and believe in God's strength. That's a combination that makes it possible to win, even with lights in clay pots.

I suppose the lessons to be learned from this story are fairly transparent. We don't need a New Testament interpretation of these verses in order to discern how the lessons can be applied to the challenges of Christian living and Christian ministry. And indeed the New Testament makes only one passing reference to Gideon and his faith (cf. Hebrews 11:32). Or is there more, if we look a little more carefully?

I found it fascinating when I first noticed the way Paul in 2 Corinthians 4 addresses the whole issue of *weakness* and *strength* with reference to Christian ministry.

Second Corinthians portrays an apostle who looks very much like Gideon surrounded by the Midianites. He is well aware of the challenges he faces, of the enemies surrounding him, and of his own weakness. And yet in a significant passage in chapters 3 and 4 we hear a recurring refrain: "Therefore, since we have such a hope, we are very bold" (3:12) and "Therefore we do not lose heart" (4:16).

What made it possible for Paul to speak like this? I think the answer is that he understood the Gideon story and applied it to his own situation. Between these two affirmations of courage and hope we find a text that begins like this:

> For God, who said, "Let light shine out of darkness," made his light shine in our hearts. (2 Cor., 4:6a)

Paul is obviously alluding to the creation story, where God called forth light out of darkness. But he is also thinking of Gideon's story, where the lights suddenly shone in the darkness and God gave an impossibly small army an impossible victory.

God revealed his power in the beginning of creation when light first dispelled the darkness. And it happened again, when God used light in the darkness to give Gideon's army the victory over Midian. God is doing it even today, says Paul, when the light which is our knowledge of God's glory shining in Jesus' face enlightens our own dark hearts. And just to make sure that the reader's mind doesn't jump from the first creation story to the new creation story in Jesus without pausing to reflect on the Gideon story along the way, Paul makes the allusion clear:

> But we have this treasure in jars of clay. (2 Cor. 4:7a)

There can be no doubt that Paul is thinking of the Gideon story. We are ordinary breakable clay jars, and into these clay jars God shines a glorious light. And precisely because we are weak and fragile, easily cracked and broken, God can use us in order to make the light visible beyond our own hearts into the dark night of this world.

And just in case his readers still did not catch the allusions to the Gideon story, Paul hastens to make the connection even more explicit. God chose to put the light onto clay pots

> ...to show that this all-surpassing power is from God and not from us. (2 Cor. 4:7b)

That is exactly what God said to Gideon! We are never too weak to win. We are always exactly as weak as God wants us to be. God wins precisely because we are weak enough to be sure we cannot defeat our enemies in our own strength, and trusting enough to know that we can be victorious in God's. If we thought we were strong enough, God could not give us the victory. We would only think we had done it ourselves. And if we used lame excuses like, "I am too small!" and "I am too weak!" we would not be taking God's power into consideration.

By using a small army of torches and torches in breakable clay pots, God taught Israel and the Midianites whose power was at work. And by using us in our weakness, by shining the light of God's glory in and through the breakable clay pots of our own lives, God shows us and the world to whom the victory really belongs. But everything depends on our willingness to admit our weakness and trust in God's strength.

Paul goes on to describe all the things these breakable clay pots need to endure in the ministry of the Gospel (2 Cor. 4:8,9,16-18):

> We are hard pressed on every side, but not crushed; perplexed, but not in despair; persecuted, but not abandoned; struck down, but not destroyed.
>
> Therefore we do not lose heart. Though outwardly we are wasting away, yet inwardly we are being renewed day by day. For our light and momentary troubles are achieving for us an eternal glory that far outweighs them all. So we fix our eyes not on what is seen, but on what is unseen. For what is seen is temporary, but what is unseen is eternal.

The Gideon story reveals an amazing military strategy that God used over three thousand years ago. Second Corinthians 4 teaches us that this strategy is still God's way of gaining the victory.

God's strength is made perfect in weakness. God's glory and might go on display when we are willing to be small and weak and breakable, but at the same time recklessly and obediently trusting in God. God's glory is revealed most clearly when God's divine light shines into our hearts and then back out through the cracks and holes of these fragile clay pots.

No one is too weak to be used by God! No one can say that they are too small or too unknown or too ungifted. That was the first lesson

Gideon had to learn. And then he had to learn the second one: No one can think they are strong enough, or great enough, or gifted enough to win God's victory. God does not use strong and gifted people when they think their own strength is great enough. Otherwise we might boast and say we did it in our own strength! (Judges 7:2)

We're exactly as weak as God wants us to be. How else will people ever discover that "this extraordinary power belongs to God and does not come from us"?

Gideon's excuses were: "I'm too small! I'm too weak!" What are ours? Perhaps: "I don't have any great spiritual gifts;" or "I don't have enough training;" or "I'm too young;" or "I'm too old;" or "I'm too busy;" "If only I were bigger, or stronger, or older, or had more experience, or more time!" And God says, "When you are weak, then I am strong" – "It is not by might, nor by power, but by my Spirit" – "My power is made perfect in weakness."

Where Will We Fix Our Eyes?

2 Kings 2:1-15

The story of Elijah and the fiery chariot and horses is well known. It is a story with the power to stir up human imagination and creativity. I still remember the children's Bible I used when I was young. My favorite picture was the one where an old man with a long beard stood with up-raised arm in a fiery chariot pulled by wild, fiery horses taking off into a stormy sky. I remember trying in vain to reproduce this picture with crayons in my Sunday school class.

Those of us who enjoy classical music probably know the *Elijah* by Mendelssohn. At the appropriate place in this oratorio, the choir sings in a *forte*, accompanied by cymbals and trumpets: "There came a fiery chariot, with fiery, fiery horses, and he went by a whirlwind to heaven."

And of course we know the spiritual, where there are no cymbals and no trumpets. Instead, in gentle, swaying music, comes the fervent prayer for deliverance: "Swing low, sweet chariot, comin' for to carry me home!"

It's such a well-known story, such a gripping story. Things happen. It's perfect for children's Bibles, for songs, for poetry. *But what in the world does it mean?*

For me it has always been an interesting and rewarding challenge to take a new look at those old, well-known Bible stories that we've known since childhood: stories that captivated us then, stories we drew in our coloring books, but stories we might never have thought deeply about.

The important question we need to ask when we look at any Biblical text is the question, "What are we supposed to learn from the story?" What if we posed this question to the story of Elijah and the fiery chariot and horses?

The answer is by no means self-evident. We are surely not being taught to follow Elijah's example, are we? – trying to chase our servant away, miraculously parting a river, ascending to heaven in a most unusual vehicle. If so, we're not doing so well at it!

But surely we're not being taught to be like Elisha either, are we? – disobeying our master, begging parting blessings, watching intently as he's whisked away from us, using his fallen clothes to do miracles. If so, we're not doing well at that, either.

I'm going to take the risk of interpreting the story of Elijah's ascent into heaven in a way that is probably quite different than what you have heard before. It's not my aim to be controversial or provocative. It's just that something happened when I first took a good long look at this text and kept probing it with one crucial question: "What in the world are we supposed to learn from this text?"

This story contains a number of puzzling features. And yet I want to propose that it is worth our while to work at the puzzles until the meaning and the challenge of the story begin to emerge.

I'll give you the punch line first and tell you what I think this story is teaching. But then I want us to look more closely at the text and see *how* it teaches this lesson. Perhaps the story doesn't actually say what we've often thought it said.

I believe this story wants to teach us one of the key answers to this question:

> *Under what condition can I expect to live in the power of the Spirit of God, the way Elijah and Elisha did?*

Now, the issue here is not *how* the power and presence of God's Spirit will be manifested in our lives. The issue is not whether we can divide the Jordan River miraculously as these men did. It's not about miracles, nor about becoming prophets. God works in many ways, and will likely work in and through us differently than happened in the lives of Elijah and Elisha.

This text is not about *how* the Spirit will work in and through us. It is about *what needs to happen in us* – what priorities we need to have, what choices we need to make – so that God's Spirit can be released in our lives in whatever way God chooses to do that.

I believe this story calls us to make precisely the choice that Elisha was asked to make. And it holds out the promise that if we do, then we too will have met the divine condition for walking in the power of God's Spirit.

The story indicates rather clearly which choice Elisha had to make if he wanted to inherit the spirit of Elijah – that is, the Spirit of God that had been at work in Elijah. Let's read the text:

> Elijah said, "Tell me, what can I do for you before I am taken from you?"
>
> Elisha answered, "Let me inherit a double portion of your spirit."
>
> Elijah responded, "You have asked a difficult thing. Yet if you see me when I am taken from you, it will be yours – otherwise not." (2 Kings 2:9,10)

Elisha was supposed to keep his eyes fixed on Elijah as he was taken away into heaven. If he would do that, then his request for the Spirit would be granted. If not, he would not get what he had requested. What a strange condition!

Try to imagine the situation. What would we expect Elisha to do? He's standing there beside his master. Suddenly a fiery chariot and horses appear and Elijah is whisked away. Would we expect him to watch? What would we do? Would we watch? Or would we perhaps notice that our shoes were untied, bend down to tie them, and accidentally miss the entire episode?

I think it would be impossible to do anything but keep our eyes glued to the amazing scene before us. How could Elisha possibly miss it? How could "watching" here be as difficult as Elijah made it out to be?

Maybe because the horses whipped up so much dust that Elisha's eyes hurt and he could hardly keep them open? Or was the fire too bright? Are we supposed to believe that Elisha was granted the Spirit of God simply because he kept his eyes open when something spectacular was happening right in front of him? If so, why would Elijah have called that a "difficult thing"?

As I've already hinted, perhaps we are not reading the story correctly. Maybe if we notice what the text *actually says*, the puzzling pieces will start to make sense.

What really happened to Elijah? According to Mendelssohn, according to the spiritual, according to all those Sunday school pictures, Elijah rode up into heaven in a fiery chariot pulled by fiery horses. That is clearly said in countless children's Bible story books. The one place where we've never found this is in the Bible. That's not what the text says at all!

Let's check out what the text says. 2 Kings 2 opens with these words:

> When the Lord was about to take Elijah up to heaven *in a whirlwind*, Elijah and Elisha were on their way from Gilgal.

And then later,

> As they were walking along and talking together, suddenly a chariot of fire and horses of fire appeared and separated the two of them, and Elijah went up to heaven *in a whirlwind*. (2:11)

Okay, how was Elijah taken up into heaven? In a fiery chariot? The text doesn't say that. Twice it says clearly that he went up in a whirlwind. Why do we always imagine that Elijah went to heaven in the chariot? Probably because we can't find any other explanation for the sudden appearance of the fiery chariot and horses.

And so we imagine that Elijah either climbs into the chariot, or is miraculously whisked up into it, and that the whirlwind in the story takes not only Elijah up to heaven, but the chariot and horses as well!

But what if we were to take seriously what the text actually says? Let's hear it one more time:

> As they were walking along and talking together, suddenly a chariot of fire and horses of fire appeared and separated the two of them, and Elijah went up to heaven in a whirlwind. (2:11)

The chariot and horses separate these two men as they are talking together. Elijah is taken up to heaven in a whirlwind. That's what the text says. And what happened to the fiery chariot and horses? We are not told. Elijah could hardly tell us – he's already been whisked away in the whirlwind. Elisha can't tell us – he wasn't watching the chariot and the horses. He kept his eyes fixed on Elijah, just as he was supposed to! The narrator doesn't tell us, because that's not the point of the story. Presumably the fiery chariot and horses drove off into the desert and disappeared.

But suddenly some lights start going on for us. The condition that Elisha had to fulfill if he wanted to receive the Spirit starts to make more sense. Perhaps we still wonder what it has to do with a spiritual blessing, but at least at the level of the narrative some pieces start coming together.

Elisha had a choice to make. There were two things vying for his attention: he could fix his eyes on Elijah who was carried off to heaven in a whirlwind, or he could be distracted by the fascinating fiery chariot and horses. Where would he fix his eyes?

Of course no one would be distracted from watching a fiery chariot and horses because of untied shoes. But think of it the other way around. Would anyone be distracted by a fascinating fiery chariot pulled by fiery horses when he is supposed to fix his gaze on something else? Easily.

So what does this have to do with a spiritual blessing? How can looking the right direction in the desert have anything to say to this question: "Under what conditions can we be filled with the power of God's Spirit?" What remains is to recognize the rich biblical symbolism conveyed through the details of this story. When this is done a challenging message begins to emerge, one addressed to all of us.

In Scripture, wind, whirlwind or storm often represent the presence of God. "His way is in the whirlwind and the storm" (Nahum 1:3). One of the main Hebrew words for "wind" is used regularly for God's Spirit in the Old Testament. And the same is true of the Greek words in the New Testament. Over and over again the Bible uses the words "wind" or "whirlwind" to refer to the power of the Spirit of God. Literally dozens of examples could be cited. We need only think of Jesus' words, "The *wind* blows where it wills . . . so it is with everyone born of the *Spirit*," (John 3:8) or of the Pentecost story, where a rushing mighty wind signals the coming of God's Spirit (Acts 2:2).

But what about "chariots and horses"? These symbolize power and might – usually human power and might, but sometimes also God's miracle-working power and protective hand. For example, they stood for the power of Egypt, as we are told that all Egypt's horses and chariots chased the fleeing Israelites (Exod. 14:23). Deuteronomy warns that the future king of Israel should not assemble horses (Deut. 17:16). But Israel didn't heed God's warning. We are told that during the time of the monarchy in Israel, they had as many as 1,400 chariots and 12,000 riders (1 Kings 10:26). But we also have God's commentary on Israel's military strength. Psalm 33:16-17 tells us:

> No king is saved by the size of his army; no warrior escapes by his great strength. A horse is a vain hope for deliverance; despite all its great strength it cannot save.

Israel did not heed the warning. The more horses and chariots they assembled, the more they trusted in these to save them, and the less they put their hope in God. Horses and chariots often represent the temptation to trust in human strength instead of the power of the God of Israel.

Over and over the people of Israel had to make the same choice. Where would they put their trust? Where would they fix their eyes? Where would they find their security? In human power and might? In their own abilities? In their military possibilities? In their political alliances? Or would they put their trust in God? Would they find their ultimate security in the power of God's Spirit?

Elijah had learned to live in the power of God's Spirit. Now it was this Spirit, made visible in the whirlwind, that carried Elijah up to heaven. Elisha was called to "See this!" – to see this with eyes that *really see*! But there was also a great temptation to miss it, a temptation to be distracted, to be drawn away by the symbols of human power and might. What a spectacular sight those fiery chariots and horsemen must have been! How easily they could have drawn Elisha's attention away from the power of God.

But there is another side to the story as well. In terms of his dependence on God's mighty strength rather than on human power, Elijah had been a model in his life and ministry. What Elijah had to learn, however, is that ultimately God's own person and presence, the Spirit of the living God, must be our focus. That is where we must fix our eyes ... not only the signs and wonders that sometimes flow from God's mighty hand.

That was a hard lesson for Elijah to learn. As long as Elijah's prayers called forth a punishing drought and afterward a mighty cloudburst – as long as he could call down fire from heaven – Elijah was courageous and strong. But as soon as the stream of miracles ceased, as soon as Elijah discovered he had powerful enemies and that they were after his life, everything changed. Then we read: "He was afraid. He got up and fled for his life." Not long after we see him lying under a broom tree, depressed and wishing to die (1 Kings 19:3,4).

God met the troubled Elijah at Mt. Horeb, but did so in a special way, so that Elijah would learn one of life's most important lessons. First God sent a powerful storm that tore the mountains apart and shattered the rocks. After that came an earthquake, then a great fire: just what Elijah imagined should accompany the coming of God. But God was not present in any of these spectacular events. God came quietly; God spoke in a still, small voice. And Elijah learned his lesson. God's presence was revealed, not only in power and might, not only in signs and wonders, not only in cloudbursts and fire from heaven. God is also present, God's Spirit is our companion, even if all we hear is God's quiet whisper.

Elisha needed to learn this same lesson. He, too, would experience great signs and wonders; indeed twice as many miracles of Elisha are reported in Scripture as of Elijah before him. On one occasion he is even given a vision of nothing other than *fiery chariots and horses*, sent to guarantee Israel God's protection against the chariots and horses of the Arameans (2 Kings 6:17). Now, before his ministry begins, Elisha is given a test. Where will he fix his eyes? What will be his highest priority? Will it be in horses and chariots, or will it be the Spirit of God? Signs and wonders are not the bottom line, nor are power and might, certainly not *human* power and might. The correct focus is God – God's person and presence. That is where true help and security lie.

Elijah had warned Elisha that his request was a difficult one. Do we see the magnitude of the decision Elisha was called to make? He couldn't have both: either he would fix his eyes upon the chariots and horsemen, or on the whirlwind taking his master to heaven. Either he would fix his eyes on the symbols of power and might (whether these be human or divine), or else he would fix them on the Spirit of God.

Elisha passed the test. He made the right decision. He refused to be distracted. And so, as Elijah was disappearing into heaven, Elisha cried out: "My Father, My Father. The chariots and horsemen of Israel" (cf. 2 Kings 13:14).

He was not saying, "Look Elijah, you are sitting in a chariot!" Nor was he saying, "Look over there, Elijah! Look at the fiery chariot and horses going by!" No. Elisha was making a confession of faith when he said, "My Father: The chariots and horsemen of Israel." He was saying, as it were: "Father Elijah, now I understand. The *true* chariots and horses – the true power and security in difficult times – is the Spirit of God; it is the Spirit that was at work in your life and that now leads you to your reward."

Elisha had stood the test. He had proven himself ready to be filled with the power of God's Spirit.

How about us? Aren't we also called to make the decision Elisha made? Aren't we often overly fascinated and impressed with human achievements – tempted to put our hopes in human strength, human ingenuity, human methods? If we reckon with divine intervention, then it must be something spectacular, something unmistakable. It's not easy to keep our eyes fixed on the ways of God's Spirit or to recognize that the "true chariots and horsemen of Israel" are to be found in those who, like Elijah, live in the presence of God as they invest their lives in the work of God.

This story holds out a challenge for us, but also a great promise. It says what the rest of the Bible also says – that living in the fullness of God's Spirit is far less an esoteric inner spiritual experience than we sometimes imagine. Living by God's Spirit means experiencing God's presence and going about God's business, as Elijah did. We are not filled by God's Spirit because we have practiced the right rituals, fasted long enough, or prayed in a special way. We do not live by the Spirit of God because we have reached some high plateau of spiritual maturity or mystical communion with God. We live in the presence of God's Spirit as we join with those who choose God and who learn to walk in God's ways, who draw on divine resources.

God's Spirit is present for those who are not distracted by symbols of human achievement that aim to glorify the human agent rather than the divine enabler. God's Spirit lifts up the weak and the fallen when their hope is in God and not in the chariots and horses.

In times of sadness, where will our hearts find renewed joy? In times of temptation, where will we find courage to withstand? In times of doubt, where will we find renewed hope and faith? In times of financial or personal insecurity, where will we find a solid rock? When we need to make important decisions, where will we seek guidance? When the assignments overwhelm us, from where will the endurance and the faithfulness come? We often face the temptation to trust in our own strength, our own ingenuity, our own plans and preparations, even when the challenges are far bigger than our abilities. Or we hope for a spectacular miracle and wonder where God is when none is given.

The story of Elijah and the fiery chariot and horses calls us to do the one thing that is necessary in order that we might find all the necessary resources in God – and that is to *choose God*, to rely on God, to trust in God's Spirit and presence to be our guide and help and hope and strength.

All around us are "chariots and horses" that are trying to steal our attention, to distract us from the presence of God. We find these chariots and horses in our society, in our places of work, in our homes, even in our churches. And they often lead us into temptation. But God is there too, calling us to focus our attention on the one who will never leave us nor forsake us, calling us to hear once again the words: "It is not by might, nor by power, but by my Spirit, says the Lord Almighty" (Zech. 4:6).

Love Your Enemies!

Matthew 5:38-48

"You have heard that it was said, 'Eye for eye, and tooth for tooth.' But I tell you, Do not resist an evil person. If someone strikes you on the right cheek, turn to him the other also. And if someone wants to sue you and take your tunic, let him have your cloak as well. If someone forces you to go one mile, go with him two miles. Give to the one who asks you, and do not turn away from the one who wants to borrow from you.

"You have heard that it was said, 'Love your neighbor and hate your enemy.' But I tell you: Love your enemies and pray for those who persecute you, that you may be sons of your Father in heaven. He causes his sun to rise on the evil and the good, and sends rain on the righteous and the unrighteous. If you love those who love you, what reward will you get? Are not even the tax collectors doing that? And if you greet only your brothers, what are you doing more than others? Do not even pagans do that? Be perfect, therefore, as your heavenly Father is perfect."

Mark Twain once said, "It ain't those parts of the Bible that I can't understand that bother me, it is the parts that I do understand."

This text from Matthew 5:38-48 is one of those texts that seem to speak pretty clearly. There are not a lot of complicated sentences; there's no difficult theological vocabulary; there are no parables that sound really mysterious; there are no references to obscure people and places and objects. It just tells us how to live:

- Don't retaliate;
- Be willing to suffer persecution and insult;
- Be willing to be cheated both in court and out of it;
- Willingly do more for others than they even demand;
- Lend generously to anyone, even if you know you won't get your stuff back;
- Love friends and enemies alike; pray for everyone;
- Greet family and strangers and your sworn enemies with a friendly greeting;
- Bottom line: Just be perfect. God is!

Now what could be easier to understand than that? And what could be more hopelessly impossible to actually do than that? And precisely because the text seems to describe such an impossible ideal, the scholars have gotten to work on it and asked all sorts of difficult questions that have made it, in the end, not only difficult to do but also difficult to understand.

Some say: "That is such an unrealistic set of instructions. It could not possibly have been meant for normal living. They must have been Jesus' special instructions for the disciples when he sent them on their preaching mission in Galilee, so that they would know how to deal with situations of persecution. It's obviously not for normal people in normal circumstances."

Some say: "Well, you can't run a society on principles like that! Obviously, it is meant for a temporary situation where a crisis is on the horizon and heroic actions are needed for a short period of time – as in the crisis of Jesus' ministry, and perhaps in subsequent crises like when Ghandi tried to persuade Britain to change policies in India, or when Martin Luther King raised awareness of civil rights issues. But these principles cannot possibly work in normal life."

Some say: "These instructions are for an ideal world, the kind of world that will exist after Jesus sets up his thousand year reign of peace on earth. Someday the world will be the kind of place where these instructions can be taken seriously and practiced literally. After all, it's a lot easier to turn the second cheek if nobody is hitting the first one, to lend if nobody has any needs anymore, and to pray for those who persecute you when persecution is a thing of the past!"

Some say: "This has nothing to do with how we live in the world. It has to do with Christian relationships. In the world we live by the rules that make sense in the world:

- We retaliate, though we usually do it through legal channels, using the court system to get what we deserve and to make sure our enemies get what they deserve. There must be justice, after all;
- We insult back when people insult us – or at least we make sure we stay clear of people who insult us;
- We make sure we take care of ourselves and of our families first!
- We don't lend out anything we can't be sure of getting back, and of course we take security deposits before lending anything to strangers;
- We love our friends and make sure we keep a good distance from our enemies;
- And that part about being perfect like God is? Well, God's perfection sometimes expresses itself in wrath and justice and punishment of the wicked – sometimes even in the death penalty.

In the *church*, perhaps, we are willing to suffer wrong, but not out there in the big bad world. It just would not make any sense!"

Finally, some say: "Of course we cannot fulfill the impossible ideals of the Sermon on the Mount. Who knows that better than God? And that is the point of it all. He puts up an impossible ideal, we fail, and then we run to God for mercy. After all, the Christian life is about forgiveness and grace, not about living rightly. Nobody lives rightly. The more impossible the ideal, the quicker we realize how utterly incapable we are of living the Christian life, and the sooner we find refuge in Jesus who lived the Christian life for us and simply asks us to accept his perfection by faith."

Well, by the time the scholars are finished with a text like this, the clear crystal waters of a challenging text have been stirred and muddied and mixed with enough theological theory that we cannot see anything clearly anymore! And so we just tuck it away and say: "That's one of those difficult texts; we'd like to take it seriously but we just don't really know what it means."

Let me suggest that there are indeed some things that we *can* know clearly about this text. I suggest the following four points.

1. This is not an ethic for the world

Jesus was not trying to set up some kind of utopian society, trying to enforce heavenly standards through an earthly political or legal system.

He intended to transform the world by establishing an alternative society that lived by different values. That is why Jesus addresses this sermon, not to the crowds, but to his disciples. The crowds are there and they are listening in, but Jesus is talking to the disciples (Matt. 5:1-2).

Only at the end of the sermon does Jesus acknowledge that the crowd is listening in. Indeed, he makes his final comments to his disciples with that crowd in mind, confronting the crowd with the decision they must now make. Will they build their house on the sand? Will they listen to Jesus' discipleship teaching and then leave without committing themselves to Jesus' way? Or will they build their house on the rock by saying "yes" to Jesus, by saying "yes" to what he has taught his disciples – "yes," not in word, but in deed, in the concrete act of joining those who have stepped out of the crowd and now stand among the committed?

Jesus makes it clear that to be his disciples involves much more than "accepting Christ's perfection by faith." Jesus insists that discipleship includes hearing his words and acting on them (7:24). That is precisely what "the crowd" will not do. That is what disciples do. The crowds were astounded by Jesus' teaching. They were amazed at Jesus' authority. But amazement was not enough. In the end, each person in the crowd was confronted with the decisive question: "Will I be a doer, and not only a hearer? Will I step out of the crowd and join the circle of disciples?"

The entire sermon is about how *disciples of Jesus* are to live. The Sermon on the Mount is not an ethic for the world! It was not designed to be a proposal about how a worldly society should organize itself. Thus Jesus' sermon does not mean that the world must:

- get rid of the justice system (Why not just pray for evildoers?)
- get rid of the police force (Who needs it if we'd rather be hit twice than stop the criminal?)
- get rid of small claims courts (What's wrong with being cheated?)
- get rid of the army (We'll just let the enemies overrun our nation! After all, we love them!)

The Sermon on the Mount does not prescribe an ethic for the world.

Now that does not mean that the world would not *benefit* if it adopted many of the principles of the Sermon on the Mount! Of course it would. The world would benefit greatly by taking to heart a whole series of the insights and instructions of the sermon. But Jesus calls for choice. He does not impose his ethic on those who have not chosen him. And he did not come to abolish the kingdoms of this world – not yet, at any rate. He came to gather a community that would join with him and with each other in living in this world according to the principles of the Kingdom of God. They will be out of step with the world's way of doing things, but they will be a sign that God's perfect plan is completely different than anything that can be imposed by force or by law or by armies in a sinful world.

Jesus did not expect the world to act Christianly. He came to call Christians to act differently from the world!

2. This is an ethic for the Christian community

Jesus *did* mean for people to take the instructions in this text seriously and practice them in life, but he meant for his *disciples* to do so. They are the ones who have committed themselves to hear Jesus' words and put them into practice – like the wise man building his house on the rock. And these are his instructions. These are the things he intends us to put into practice.

This is an ethic for the Christian community; it is not an ethic just for individual Christians to practice in the realm of their own private personal piety. Every line in these instructions is about relationships between people! What sense does it make to say: "Yes, I am committed to live by the Sermon on the Mount – but only in my private life"? In my private life no one ever hits my cheek or sues me for my shirt. In my private life no one ever forces me to help them or acts like an enemy. These things only happen in my relationships with other people.

Moreover, it is only in community that we find the support and encouragement we need to take courageous steps toward living the ideals of this passage. I can refuse retaliation if I know that I have a supportive Christian community surrounding me and supporting my decision. My Christian brothers and sisters might even be willing to step in and speak to the enemy or at least to comfort the victim. It is a lot harder to do all this alone.

3. The Christian community that lives like this does so also in relation to the world

I said this is an ethic for Christians, not for the world. But that does not mean that we live this way in the church, and then live as the world does when we are in the world. We are called to live like God in an ungodly world. We are called to live self-sacrificially in a world that wants to take advantage of us for it. And the persecution and insults that this text talks about – well, I hope I am right in assuming that most of that happens *outside*, not *inside*, the community of faith.

The Sermon on the Mount describes how Christians live in their relationships with each other, but also how they live in their relationships with people in the world. That is what God does: God sends rain on the evil and on the good; God sends the sun to shine on the righteous and the unrighteous. That is the whole point of the passage.

Jesus said: "If you love those who love you, what reward do you have? Do not even the tax collectors do the same? And if you greet only your brothers and sisters, what more are you doing than others? Do not even the Gentiles do the same?" We will surely be living out of step with the world if we live in the world according to the principles of the Sermon on the Mount, but that is precisely what Jesus is calling us to do. We are out of step with the world, because the world is out of step with God.

Now I hope that this next point will not cause us all to breathe a sigh of relief and quickly forget about points one through three:

4. Not everything in the Sermon on the Mount is to be taken literally

That is pretty obvious in some places. Does Jesus *really* mean that people who have trouble with lust should cut out their right eye? Of course he does: he *really* means it, but he does not mean it *literally* (as though we could not lust with our left eye!). Are Christians *really* supposed to chop off their right hand if they commit a sin with it? Yes, indeed – but not *literally*!

Jesus intended the entire sermon to be taken with utter seriousness, but not always with absolute literalness. Cutting out the eye and the hand really means being so committed to a pure life that we are ready and willing to cut ourselves off from those things that bring temptations too difficult for us to resist and from those things that put us in compromising situations where sin is just the natural next step. We take it absolutely seriously, but not always exactly literally.

There are times when in this world we do rely on a police force and a justice system and laws that work to protect us from wrongdoers. But as we have opportunity, we show by our lives, our attitudes, and our prayers where our real priorities lie. We care about those who mistreat us. We show them acts of love where we can. If we must rely on the world's anti-crime tactics, we do so not primarily to protect ourselves, but to help the world become a safer place, a place where loving the enemy can be practiced even more radically.

But this raises a difficult and much debated question: How literally do we take the "love your enemy" command when it comes to the military?

What should be the Christian's answer when called to serve in a national army? Do Christians learn from Jesus to love and pray for their enemies and at the same time from their commanding officer how to resist and kill them? Or should Christians not be in the military at all? When Jesus spoke of loving enemies, did he include "national enemies?"

I come from a tradition that takes non-participation in the military far more seriously as a Christian option than most of the Christian world does. In fact my ancestors were persecuted for refusing to join the military. My great-grandfather was shot at point-blank range, in the presence of his wife and children, because he refused to take up arms for his country.

If your viewpoint on this is different from mine, I hope you don't hear me saying that I question the seriousness of your Christian faith or the carefulness of your reasoning. No, I am just saying that I disagree with you.

There are four answers I would give to someone who asked me why I would not join the military, and in particular that part of the military that produces and uses, or supports those who produce and use, weapons of destruction.

1. I can better testify that my real allegiance is to God's Kingdom if I refuse to pledge ultimate allegiance to one of the kingdoms of this world

I want to live for God's Kingdom and if necessary to die for it. Would I be willing to *live and die* for something that is a lower priority than God's Kingdom, perhaps for an earthly kingdom? I do not know. I know that some people are willing to do so. But to *kill* for an earthly kingdom, that is another matter altogether. God is building an international and interracial church. As Christians, we belong to a world-wide family; we are bound together with all our brothers and sisters by our one Father. For me it follows that my ultimately loyalty can never belong to one of the kingdoms of this world – not to my homeland, not to my nation, not to any other geographical or political entity. And when one of these kingdoms demands my ultimate loyalty, my answer is "No." Ultimately, my loyalty belongs to God and to God's world-wide family. No kingdom of this world dare become as important to me as my brothers and sisters, who live in every part of the world. If they do, my priorities are wrong.

2.   I would not want to risk killing fellow Christians in the name of my country

Of course we would like to respond: "The Christians are on our side. That's why we fight – to stop the evil on the other side." Ah, if only that were true! In every war that has ever been fought in modern his-tory there have been Christians on both sides. And usually both sides have claimed that their side represented the justice of God.

Mennonite Central Committee put out a powerful poster with this simple message: "A modest proposal for peace: Let the Christians of the world agree that they will not kill each other." If we took that fairly modest proposal seriously, no Christian would ever join either side, lest perhaps a Christian might also join the other side!

3. I would also not want to risk killing a fellow human be-ing who is not a Christian, and thereby eliminate any pos-sibility of that person coming into a relationship with Jesus Christ

Is it so much nobler to kill someone who is not a Christian than one who is, especially given the fact that God loves all equally and that Christ died for all? Though it may be that from an earthly perspec-tive the other person truly is an enemy, we need to be clear that this justifies nothing in the sight of God. We were God's enemies when God invested everything to win us back into friendship. How desperately our world needs examples of people who are willing to live the life that God in Christ modeled for us – to love our enemies, whether personal or national. If Christians won't be those models, who will? We do not ask how lovable the enemy is, or for that matter how dangerous. We ask God how to treat enemies. God tells us, and God shows us.

My fourth reason for refusing military participation is the one I personally find most persuasive of all:

4. I believe the New Testament teaches that Jesus' own attitude to violence, when he himself was being treated unjustly, mocked, and finally crucified, is the model he asks Christians to adopt

Jesus prayed for his enemies and we are to do the same. He could have appealed to God to send twelve legions of angels to defend him, but he chose to suffer rather than inflict injury on others. And the New Testament says that when Jesus went the way of selfless suffering, he was "leaving you an example, so that you should follow in his steps … When he was abused, he did not return abuse; when he suffered, he did not threaten; but he entrusted himself to the one who judges justly" (1 Peter 2:21,23). The New Testament teaches us to follow Jesus' example.

But many Christians respond: "Of course I would be willing to sacrifice my life, but I am not willing to sacrifice my wife and my children, my neighbors, my country. If I fight the enemy, it is not to protect myself but to protect the innocent! I am acting as God's agent to defend the helpless in the face of an enemy attack."

Now, that sounds very self-sacrificial, but it does not correspond to what Jesus taught, nor to what he practiced. Jesus did indeed stand on the side of the helpless, the victims, the vulnerable. But he never resorted to violence to defend them. Indeed he went the way of the cross precisely because he chose the route of nonviolent resistance to corrupt power structures. Jesus refused to call down twelve legions of angels that would have been at his disposal to protect him. Jesus did not allow his disciples to fight on his behalf. He was revealing the truth about God's way in the world: God does not use military might to protect the innocent sufferer, not now that the Prince of Peace has come!

In every century since Jesus' day, the innocent have suffered. Indeed, dedicated followers of Jesus have suffered at the hands of vicious enemies. How often has God sent those twelve legions of angels to protect them with military might? Never. God chose not to defend Jesus with military power, and God has chosen not to defend Jesus' followers with military power; nor has God commissioned earthly armies to do so on God's behalf. God's way is the way of loving the enemy and if necessary, dying in the process. That is what Jesus did. Jesus' victory came in weakness, not in power. And we are called to follow in his steps.

Jesus did not come to set up a worldly kingdom, but to testify to the reality of a different Kingdom. He calls Christians to do the same. When we adopt the world's methods of defending worldly kingdoms, it becomes very difficult for the world to get his message. And so we choose, if necessary, to die at the hands of our enemies rather than for them to die at our hands.

A concluding story

It was the sixteenth century. A group of radical reformers, a tiny minority in their day, aimed to follow Jesus faithfully, even when that led to conflict with ecclesiastical and worldly authorities. Among those who suffered for their faith was a Christian leader named Michael Sattler. His story was portrayed in a film called *The Radicals*.

I had been deeply moved by the film version of Michael Sattler's life and witness. He and others around him were prepared to suffer unbelievably for their convictions and for confessing Jesus Christ. These predecessors of Mennonites and other Free Church traditions were models when it came to confessing Jesus in an intolerant world.

A short time later I recommended this film in a church. A man confronted me afterward with a question that got me thinking. He asked, "Would you be willing today to allow yourself to be killed because of your beliefs about baptism?" My first reaction was, "No, I would not. I know what I believe about baptism, but to make it a life and death issue, to die for it? I don't think so."

But his question and my answer troubled me. I asked myself, "For what exactly were the early Anabaptists willing to be martyred? Was it really for their convictions about baptism?" No, it wasn't quite that simple.

They died because they were convinced that true faith can never be promoted nor defended with the sword. And because they refused to take up arms against their enemies, they were vulnerable to death at the hands of their enemies. They died because they were convinced, as was Jesus, that faith convictions cannot be promoted or defended with the sword. The early Anabaptists rejected violence, and like Jesus before them died for their convictions.

Now, what if the man had formulated his question differently? What if he had asked: "What if you had to choose between two churches? In one church people were willing to die for their convictions. In the other, people were willing to kill for their convictions. Which church would you choose?" If that had been the question, then I hope I would have decided along with Michael Sattler. Thank God this is a decision that most of us are not required to make today. Our time is less life-threatening *for us*. We simply have to decide whether we will help defend an earthly kingdom with deadly force or whether we will follow Christ, the Prince of Peace.

How Does Jesus Treat Tax Collectors?

Matthew 9:9-13; 18:17

One day I set out to prepare a sermon on Matthew 9:9-13. I thought it was a nice, safe text. Matthew, the tax collector, sits at his tax collecting booth, hears Jesus summon him to follow, leaves all, and then throws a big party to celebrate. A nice safe text about open-hearted Jesus and responsive Matthew, the person who first invented party evangelism.

But working with the text got me deeper into the issue of "tax collector" than I anticipated, and led me on to other texts. And so a sermon that was supposed to be about party evangelism ended up being about ethics and discernment and the challenge of following Jesus in a pluralistic world, and sometimes a pluralistic church. My sermon that day ended up being something like this.

> As Jesus went on from there, he saw a man named Matthew sitting at the tax collector's booth. "Follow me," he told him, and Matthew got up and followed him.
>
> While Jesus was having dinner at Matthew's house, many tax collectors and "sinners" came and ate with him and his disciples. When the Pharisees saw this, they asked his disciples, "Why does your teacher eat with tax collectors and 'sinners'?"
>
> On hearing this, Jesus said, "It is not the healthy who need a doctor, but the sick. But go and learn what this means: 'I desire mercy, not sacrifice.' For I have not come to call the righteous, but sinners." (Matthew 9:9-13)

Rejected

Matthew knew all about rejection. He was a tax collector. We are not talking about some cushy job at the Internal Revenue Service building, just down the street from where I work. We are talking about the sort of tax collectors that were utterly hated by virtually all Jews in the Roman-occupied Palestine of the first century. These were people administering a very oppressive and unfair system of taxation on a conquered people. And when *Jews* worked as tax collectors they were doubly hated, for being tax collectors and for being traitors (collaborators with the occupying power) – triply hated, because the way the system worked, it fostered corruption of every sort possible – quadruply hated, because they were ceremonially unclean, always dealing with foreigners and with unclean products that had to be taxed.

So Matthew was a tax collector. That meant everyone knew he was a traitor, a dishonest man, unclean, unscrupulous – scum! And so the labels were invented. People to be despised and rejected were called "Tax Collectors and Sinners" or "Gentiles and Tax Collectors" or "Tax Collectors and Prostitutes."

Everything in the Jewish religious culture of the day said: If you are a tax collector, you are not one of us. You are guilty because of your choices, your loyalties, your character, the company you keep. You are guilty by association, if nothing else. *Oh yes, Matthew knew all about rejection!*

Accepted

But Matthew also learns about acceptance. Can you imagine what it means to Matthew when Jesus, the one whose teaching, whose deeds of mercy, whose works of power, whose message of hope is the talk of the town – when this Jesus sees Matthew sitting at the toll both and says to him, "Hey, Matthew, good to see you! How's your day been? Man, I have an offer and an invitation for you. How would you like to become one of my disciples? I'd love to have you. Come, follow me!"

"Okay," says Matthew, "I'm coming!" And he walks away from his former life, too dumb-founded to figure out which was the bigger miracle: that he would say yes, or that Jesus would invite him in the first place. Can you imagine the transformation in Matthew's life? One day a hated unclean dishonest collaborating tax collector, the next day a disciple of Jesus, learning what it means to be a faithful participant in the Kingdom of God.

So Matthew throws a party! I suppose he says to himself: "If Jesus can accept me, I guess he'll accept pretty much anybody." He orders the tri-tip, throws together the salads, and gathers his friends, "Tax Collectors and Sinners" (they are called) – and of course Jesus, the center of the celebration – and of course a few former fishermen, who have no choice but to accept Matthew into the group; after all, they don't get to decide. Jesus does!

The Pharisees are incensed. But their complaints just give Jesus the perfect occasion to explain that it is precisely people like Matthew that he is most eager to reach with the good news, and that mercy and not religiosity pleases God.

So we know about Matthew. We know about his former life as a rejected tax collector and what that meant. We know about his new life as an accepted and beloved disciple of Jesus. We know about his desire that other people come to know Jesus. He wanted them to meet the man who had accepted him and transformed his life, so that theirs could be transformed by Jesus as well.

This "tax collector-accepting Jesus"

But what else do we know about Matthew? Well, we know that he was an *author*, or at least he became one. Anyone know which is his most famous book? Of course we do. It is not some quirky coincidence that our text is about a man whose name is Matthew and it just happens to be recorded in a book by the same name! This is the same man. The man who knew all about rejection and learned all about acceptance, this man later wrote one of the foremost Gospels to introduce this "tax collector-accepting Jesus" to everyone who would read it.

Given that, wouldn't it be interesting to check what else Matthew the (former) tax collector has to say about tax collectors in his own book? Now, I always knew that Luke's Gospel highlighted tax collectors – like Zaccheus, the little man with the big heart; like the humble man whose prayer in the temple was heard by God while the prayer of the Pharisee who despised him never made it as high as the temple walls.

But I had never bothered to check whether Matthew's Gospel has a unique emphasis on tax collectors. It does indeed. After telling his own conversion story in chapter 9, Matthew provides a list of the twelve disciples in chapter 10. His list completely ignores the former professions of the others. He supplies only his own! "Simon, Andrew, James, John,

Philip, Bartholomew, Thomas, Matthew (*the tax collector*), and so on." (10:2-4) I think decades later, he still couldn't get over it!

And then in chapter 11, Matthew tells us that even the enemies of Jesus sometimes get it right. They accuse Jesus of being "a friend of tax collectors and sinners." Of course they think they are discrediting Jesus, but Jesus quotes them, as if to say, "That's who I am!" and Matthew records the incident as if to say, "You bet, he sure is!"

How to treat a tax collector

And then comes the text in Matthew 18, a text that has been so terribly misunderstood. Matthew 18 defines church and challenges the church. It calls us to model ourselves after humble children, to exercise great care not to offend those weak in the faith, to deal with sin and temptation in our own lives. It tells how much God cares for each individual, picturing God as a happy shepherd who has just found his lost sheep. (And I bet the parties in heaven make Matthew's celebration look like a feeble practice run.)

It's a chapter that calls us to forgive seventy times seven, that promises Heaven will confirm what we "bind" and "loose" on earth, that assures us Jesus is present when we gather in his name to be about his business.

And in the middle of this chapter is the so-called "Rule of Christ" (as the early Anabaptists called it), a set of instructions designed to help the church respond when members fall into sin. There are four steps, each of them aiming at restoration. First one person tries, then one or two more get involved, then the whole church does, and if everything fails, the final step is taken.

Throughout the history of the Anabaptist movement, that final step took various forms. Sometimes it was excommunication; sometimes it was shunning, exercising the so-called "ban." Often the whole approach deteriorated into a perfunctory attempt to work through the three pre-conditions necessary before the church gained the right to come down hard on the offender. Often the whole set of procedures was administered legalistically and unlovingly. In recent decades the "Rule of Christ" has itself fallen under the ban. Most churches would not want to touch the topic with a ten-foot pole.

So why do I draw this text into a study of Matthew the tax collector, and on the themes of rejection and acceptance? Because right in the middle of Matthew 18, the word "tax collector" shows up again.

Matthew, the converted tax collector turned author, has already shown us what *Jesus* does with tax collectors – he invites them, accepts them, eats with them, chooses them. Now Matthew wants to teach *the church* what to do with tax collectors. And so we read:

> "If the offender refuses to listen even to the church, let such a one be to you as a Gentile and a tax collector." (18:17 NRSV)

So what should the church do with tax collectors? Ban them? Excommunicate them? Shun them?

Where did we ever get the idea that this is what the Rule of Christ is all about? Whatever led anyone to conclude that when Matthew, *who knows how Jesus treats tax collectors*, would write, "Treat him like a Gentile and a Tax Collector," he means, "Get him out of here! Have nothing to do with him!"? I think it means exactly the opposite. I think it means, "Love him! Accept him! Invite him! Eat with him! And keep on challenging him to be transformed into a faithful disciple of Jesus!"

And how could "Treat him like a Gentile" mean "Get rid of him!" Reject him! Shun him!" in a Gospel that ends with Jesus' commission to invite into the fellowship of Jesus Gentiles from every nation on earth?

When Matthew writes, "Treat him like a tax collector," he surely means, "Treat him the way Jesus treated me. He loved me, accepted me, invited me!" When Matthew writes, "Treat him like a Gentile," he surely means, "Go to the ends of the earth to win him back into a life of discipleship."

Defining our sins

But now we come to some tough questions. What if we cannot be sure what exactly constitutes "sin" in specific situations? What if some think there is a sinner to be restored, and others think nothing is being done wrong?

Let's ask the question this way. What happens to "tax collectors" when they are accepted by Jesus? Well we know what happened to Matthew. He *stopped* being a tax collector and *started* to be a disciple. His profession did not disqualify him from being loved, accepted and invited. But when he responded to Jesus, he *left* his profession! And so did Simon and Andrew when Jesus called them from their fishing nets.

But what about Zaccheus? He was another tax collector whom Jesus loved, and accepted and invited. Only as far as we know, he never left his profession. Salvation came to his house and he just kept right on being a tax collector, only now he became an honest one, and a generous one.

You see there are two possibilities for tax collectors who are accepted by Jesus. You either trade in your life of tax collecting for a new profession as a follower of Jesus, or you start to collect taxes "Christianly." It was the same with fishermen. Jesus called four of them to leave their nets and follow Jesus. They will no longer fish for fish; they will now fish for people. But does every fisherman have to change professions when they start following Jesus? Of course not. One can also learn to fish *"Christianly"* – no more cursing and swearing at the competition, no more use of false scales when selling the catch, no more selfish hoarding when the big catch comes in and your neighbor is starving.

But what about all the other professions? Does a Centurion who follows Jesus give up a military career and become a soldier of the cross? Or does he learn what it means to become a Christian soldier? Almost all my students at seminary assume the latter when we discuss what the New Testament teaches about participation in the military. I don't. What does a prostitute do? Jesus loves and accepts them, too. Do they learn how to *"prostitute Christianly?"* Well, hardly.

If we tried to make up lists of things to be given up by followers of Jesus, and of things to be *continued* – only done "Christianly" – we might have an easy time on some matters and some lively debates about others.

For the longest time the early church thought that being a "Gentile" had to be given up. Of course a Gentile can become a Christian, they just have to stop being Gentiles. Convert to the Jewish faith, believe in Jesus and you are in! A few decades later, but not without great pain, much discussion, serious dialog, searching of Scripture, and dependence on the Spirit, they changed their viewpoint and said, "Jesus loves and accepts you 'as a Gentile.'" You can remain a Gentile! But now you need to learn what it means to become a "Christian Gentile." There is still a former life to leave behind, a transformation process to experience, but you don't have to stop being a Gentile!

I assume that in the first century, tax collectors would normally *stop* being tax collectors, if they responded to the Gospel of Jesus (making Zaccheus an exception). In the twenty-first century, I suspect one could keep right on working for the IRS (or Revenue Canada) and faithfully follow Jesus. And what is true of professions also applies to lifestyle and ethical choices.

The church I attended in my youth decided there was no way to attend movies "Christianly." Christians did not attend movies. Over time, we, and they, learned that one can attend a movie theater "Christianly." I have lived in places where it was assumed that drinking alcohol could not be combined with a life of discipleship. In other places, my church context has believed one can drink "Christianly."

I am sure we could all make lists of debatable issues, where either the church has changed its view over time, or where churches disagree with each other, or (as is often the case these days) it is difficult in any one church to reach a consensus. Is a military career in conflict with the life of discipleship or is there a Christian way of serving in the military? Is divorce always a contradiction of the way of Jesus, or are there situations in which there is a Christian way to divorce? Is the consumption of alcohol always a contradiction of the way of Jesus, or is there a Christian way to drink, and dance, and attend the theater?

Many of us don't feel good about having so many options open. Is the Bible not clear about these things? Well, we are often convinced it is. But then we discover that others are equally convinced on the other side. And so we need to be a discerning discipleship community, as the early church was. And they were sometimes led to change their mind, and sometimes led not to! And in our own church we have sometimes been led to change our mind, and sometimes led not to! But when the questions press on us we listen to each other, study the Scriptures, examine our hearts and priorities, depend on the Spirit, and discern what God is saying. And when we do, then we respond to situations by saying either "A" or "B".

A: "We love you and accept you just as you are. But you must stop doing what you have been doing. Repent of your sin, and we will welcome you back into full fellowship with open arms."

Or

B: "We love you and accept you just as you are. You can keep right on doing what you have been doing. But remember, there is the world's way and there is the Christian way to do it. We will help you find the Christian way."

So which of these will we say? It depends on the issue, on the circumstances, on our sense of what the Scripture teaches, and what the Spirit is saying.

The final step

But we must now come back once more to Matthew 18. In the so-called "Rule of Christ," what did it mean to take that final step, the step that says, "let him be to you as a Gentile and a tax collector"?

As I read the text, that fourth step is a step of loving and welcoming the *outsider back* into the church. This is all about insiders and outsiders, not about accepting or rejecting people. We always accept the person, but we either accept the person as an insider or accept the person as an outsider. The person begins as an *insider*. First one person loves the *insider* enough to try to restore him. Then two or three love the *insider* enough to try to restore him. Then the whole church loves the *insider* enough to try to restore him.

But what if all that does not work? Well, then the church says, "You didn't respond! We tried so hard. Now we have no choice but to recognize that you are an outsider. You are an outsider like Matthew before Jesus called him. You are an outsider like a Gentile who doesn't know Jesus. *We did not excommunicate out. We recognized* that you were outside, just as the shepherd noticed a sheep had wandered away. And so now we want to win you back in! We love you. We accept you. We invite you. Come be a part of us!"

The love never stops; the desire to restore never stops; the acceptance never stops. What changes between steps three and four is that when every attempt at reconciling the *insider* fails, then we recognize the person as an *outsider* who needs to be welcomed in.

If that is what that final step means, what is it that leads to it? Here again, I am convinced that our tradition got it all wrong. Traditionally the so-called "Rule of Christ" was used to rule against those who had committed a specific sin, one of the things the church could not tolerate. When I first became a church member that list included drinking, dancing, going to movies – and in case we youth would become a bit too creative, they added "and any other questionable amusements." The list varies from church to church and it changes over time, but the church usually assumes it needs a list. How else can we decide whether the sin committed is of such a serious nature that we need to go all the way to the fourth step?

When I read Matthew 18, I see something completely different. Yes, it is about sin. And that presupposes that the church can, at least sometimes, discern what falls into the category of sin. But it is not about defining which sins are minor (and merit only the first step), which are more serious (and merit step two as well), which are even more serious (so that the whole church gets involved), and which are of such a grave nature that we consider even the fourth step, excluding from fellowship. As I read it we always start with step one and we *always* keep going until the goal of restoration is reached.

But you see, I am reading this text altogether different than some of my ancestors did. The fourth step reads like this, "If he refuses to listen even to the church, let him be to you as a Gentile and a tax collector." For what? for smoking? or drinking? or dancing? for divorcing? for adultery? for embezzling money? No – *for not listening to the church.*

This is not about "How serious was the sin?" This is about, "Is this, or is this not, the discipleship community to which I am accountable?" This text presupposes a very radical concept of the Christian fellowship, one that recognizes the presence of Jesus, not so much in the private conscience of each individual disciple, but in the gathered community discerning together the way of Jesus. There are tough decisions, but the church is equipped with the Word of God, the presence of Jesus, and the help of the Spirit, and so it can make tough decisions. And when the decisions are made, they are ratified in heaven. That does not mean they are infallible. It means that God expects us to live according to our mutually discerned convictions.

And when someone then later says: "Yes, I know that we agreed together, but I am not going to listen to the church!" then the church, filled with sorrow, says: "Then you are for us as a Gentile and a tax collector – We love you, we accept you, we invite you, but we recognize that you are opting out of this discerning fellowship. You are not acting like an insider to be reconciled, but like an outsider to be drawn back. Won't you come? Please? Won't you signal that by saying, 'I am ready to listen to the church again'? When you do, you will be brought back into the fellowship once more."

When that is what we do and say, we will be acting as Jesus did. We will be treating tax collectors as Jesus did. And (I trust), we will be celebrating a lot of parties!

The Meaning of the Feedings in Mark's Gospel

Mark 6:30-52

Maybe it was all those Hardy Boys books I read as a child. Maybe it is the Columbo and Perry Mason episodes I still enjoy. Or maybe it was even my tenth grade math teacher or my university geometry teacher who did it to me. Somehow, somewhere, I fell in love with puzzles. It is hard for me to leave an unsolved mystery alone and simply admit "I don't know!" So maybe I don't know, but that will not stop me from trying to find out.

Is it any wonder that I fell in love with the Gospel of Mark – that long neglected, then seriously misjudged and now fascinating puzzle book of the New Testament?

In Mark's Gospel, far more questions are asked than answered (see the later chapter on "Questions and Answers, Signs and Riddles"). The reader is tantalized with hints and with calls to understand, but the answers themselves are often withheld. Wherever we turn there are mysteries:

- What is the secret of the Kingdom? (4:11)
- What do the parables mean? (4:34)
- What are the signs of the End? (13:4)
- Why does Mark's Gospel end so strangely? (16:8 – actually, interpreters can't quite figure out if this really is the end; see the chapter titled "Beginning Again")

But perhaps the most puzzling riddle of them all concerns the secret meaning of the feeding miracles. In Mark 6:30-44 the feeding of the five thousand is narrated. It is followed immediately by the remarkable little episode in which Jesus walks on the water and finally calms the storm that is buffeting the disciples' boat. And then in verse 52 comes that tantalizing little clue that there is more to all this than meets the eye.

> They were completely amazed, for they had not understood about the loaves; their hearts were hardened.

Mark significantly fails to enlighten the readers as to what mysterious meaning they had failed to grasp. And because we do not know what they should have understood about the feedings, we can not be sure what amazed them about the sea-walking episode. Nor can we be sure how a better understanding of the feeding would have led to a different response when Jesus walked on the water. So the feeding of the five thousand has a mysterious meaning, but nobody seems sure what it is, except presumably Jesus and (we may suppose) Mark.

Jesus feeds another huge crowd, as we learn in Mark 8:1-10. After this second feeding miracle, the plot thickens. Jesus warns his disciples against the yeast of the Pharisees and Herod. They miss the point. Then Jesus follows up with nine consecutive questions, all leading up to the final one: "Do you still not understand?" (Mark 8:17-21; see the next chapter). The disciples know how many baskets full of leftovers were collected, but the *meaning* of the feeding miracles has somehow escaped them.

And an examination of Markan commentaries reveals that interpreters haven't fared much better. Despite numerous attempts to decode the mysterious numbers, analyze the linguistic clues, set forth the literary patterns, or read the texts in the light of Mark's concern for Gentiles, or his focus on Jesus' passion, or his teaching about the End Time, no agreement has been reached on what Mark is getting at.

But surely the even greater puzzle is why Mark kept the answer from his readers in the first place. The answer to *that* question was once considered easy. Mark was a bungler. Too naïve to have significant theological conviction, he simply compiled miscellaneous traditions and, not surprisingly, the text creaks a little. That answer will not do any more. Even those who display no reverence for Mark as sacred Scripture are now convinced that Mark was as profound a theological thinker as any of the Gospel writers (including John), and perhaps a more subtle communicator than all of them. Why did Mark not tell his readers what constituted the secret of the Kingdom, or the sign or signs of the temple's destruction and/or of the end times? Why did Mark not tell his readers what he had in mind when he called something "the beginning of the Gospel" and even more puzzling, what he means with his mysterious ending? And what in the world is the secret meaning of the feedings – the meaning Jesus' disciples missed, and still miss?

The best place to start, if we want to decipher the hidden meaning of the first feeding miracle, is in the sea-walking incident that directly follows it (Mark 6:45-52). Mark 6:52 directly links the two incidents. The disciples had failed to understand the feeding of the five thousand, and therefore they are totally amazed when Jesus comes walking to them on the lake and, in the end, stills their storm. If we can account for their amazement in the sea-walking episode, hopefully we can determine what they failed to understand about the feeding miracle.

Some have suggested the hidden meaning is straight-forward: *Jesus is ready to meet people's needs and has the power to do so.* Amazingly, the disciples experienced the feeding miracle and somehow had not realized how clearly it portrayed Jesus graciously and readily exercising his miracle-working power to aid his followers in their time of need. No wonder they were amazed when he did the very same thing when they were in need of his help crossing the sea.

But this view, I suggest, is totally at odds with a whole set of data that Mark has carefully recorded for us. If anything, the feeding miracle shows us a miracle-worker who is *reluctant* to use his special powers to aid his needy followers.

A careful look at the sea-walking episode yields a rather interesting portrait of this miracle-working Jesus. He emerges as one who exhibits, not *eagerness*, but *reluctance*, to change miraculously the disciples' circumstances. Let us look at the text, Mark 6:45-52.

Mark carefully records the time frames involved. It is in the evening that Jesus sees the disciples straining at the oars. Will he come to their aid? Not immediately, that is made clear right away. On the contrary, he goes into the hills to pray. A good guess is that he is praying for his uncomprehending and faithless disciples: praying that they might gain understanding, so that they don't need to panic every time they face a storm. It is a full nine hours later (i.e. in the fourth watch of the night) that Jesus finally comes walking on the lake. All night he knew his disciples were struggling while he prayed. Just as Jesus waited all day before feeding the multitudes (6:35), so here he waited all night before coming to his disciples' aid.

But Jesus does finally come, and here we must read the text carefully. He does not come *in order to get into their boat*. He comes *in order to walk past it!* We are so accustomed to thinking that he walked on the water in order to get into their boat that we fail to read what the text actually says. It says he intended to walk past them (6:48). The clear impression that Mark's text gives us is that he comes into their boat and calms their storm *only because* they fail to recognize him, and because his presence and their failure to recognize him cause more terror in them than the storm itself had caused.

It is here that Mark tells us about the disciples' amazement. Is it amazement that Jesus can walk on water and calm the storm? On the contrary, it is amazement that Jesus, who has the ability to do these things, should rather allow them to struggle all night without coming to their aid, and then when finally coming, would have walked right past their boat without doing a thing. What an amazing way for a miracle-worker to behave! But if they had understood the feeding miracle, it would not have amazed them. As strange as it seems, that is what the text seems to say.

Why would Jesus behave this way? Why walk past them in the storm? Is not the sheer improbability of such a scenario sufficient warrant to look for some other interpretation, despite what the text itself says?

It is not such an improbable scenario, if we see things the disciples fail to grasp. For Jesus to pass by them in their time of need *could* be interpreted as a sign of unconcern, lack of involvement, unwillingness to help. But if we notice a clear allusion to an Old Testament text here, a very different interpretation emerges.

Exodus 33:12-23 tells of a special meeting between Moses, Israel's leader, and Yahweh, Israel's God. God has commissioned Moses to lead this "stiff-necked people" (33:5) to the Promised Land, and Moses (not surprisingly) informs God that he has no intention of leading the people unless he has some assurances that he will not be doing it alone. God comes to Moses in his distress and graciously offers to pass by ("*parerchomai*"; cf. vv.19,22) in front of Moses. By doing so, God would be assuring Moses that even when times would be hard, Moses would not be leading the people alone. God would be accompanying them to the Promised Land. God does not change any circumstances for Moses; God does not huddle beside Moses in his mountain cave and make the problems disappear. Instead God "passes by," assuring Moses that on his journey, God's presence and concern and ever-present caring help will go with him, even when times are tough and the road ahead is unknown. Circumstances remain hard, but God has "passed by" and that is enough – well, not quite enough, for God does one more thing for Moses. Graciously God offers Moses, "I will cause all my goodness to pass by in front of you, and *I will proclaim my name, Yahweh, in your presence*" (33:19 NIV).

Back to Mark's story. Jesus is walking on the lake, intending to "pass by" in the presence of his terrified disciples. But they respond in terror, not recognizing that before their eyes, Jesus is passing by to assure them that he knows and cares about their troubles. The disciples can only imagine a ghost has come to terrify them further. And so in their presence, Jesus identifies himself. "It is I," he says (6:50) – or at least, that is what the disciples hear! In the original text, the words used can just as well be translated "I AM" (*ego eimi*). It is the divine name, Yahweh, which God had pronounced in Moses' presence as the glory of the Lord passed by. But the disciples are blind to Jesus' intentions and deaf to his words. They are still terrified and amazed (vv. 50,51) as Jesus abandons his original plan, climbs into their boat and calms the sea. Instead of experiencing what theologians call a divine epiphany (a glimpse of God's presence), the disciples are fearful, amazed and clueless. "They were utterly astounded, for they did not understand about the loaves, but their hearts were hardened" (6:51,52; cf. 4:41).

What causes the disciples' fear and amazement? Are they amazed that Jesus can do such amazing miracles – multiplying bread, walking on water? I don't think so. I think they are amazed that the great miracle-worker they have come to know would *refuse* to come rushing to his disciples' aid and smooth their path. They fail to see that in Jesus, their God, Yahweh, desired to pass by and speak out the divine name in their presence so that they could be filled with courage and hope, *even while battling wind and waves.*

The disciples' incomprehension leaves them more terrified in Jesus' presence than they had been in his absence. Jesus mercifully enters their boat and calms their storm. He had not intended to do so, but they had failed to understand.

If the sea-crossing episode in Mark 6 is designed to show that Jesus does not always come immediately to work a miracle for his disciples in need, what then is the meaning of the feedings that the disciples had failed to grasp? It turns out to be precisely the same. Consider these facts:

The disciples have just returned from a mission trip, exhausted and famished. They are prevented by the clamoring crowds from meeting their basic physical need for food and rest (cf. 6:30,31). Precisely because his disciples need food and rest, Jesus proposes that they accompany him to a lonely spot.

When they arrive for their intended retreat from the crowds, their plans to eat and rest are thwarted by the eager crowds who occupy Jesus' attention all day (6:32-35). Can you imagine how hungry the disciples would be by now? They come to Jesus suggesting he dismiss the crowds so that the people can go and eat (6:36). No doubt by now they could hardly wait to do the same themselves. Jesus responds first by telling *them* to feed the crowds, and then, after they protest, by telling *them* to find out how much food was available, and having *them* organize the seating arrangements for the meal. Then, after multiplying the bread, Jesus sends *the disciples* to distribute it to the hungry crowds. There is not a word about food for the famishing *disciples*!

While the crowds eat, they are busy working; and afterward, the reader is specifically told that Jesus sends them to pick up the fragments. Even then there is not a word about their own food, though one can hardly doubt that by this time they are ready to dig into it, with or without a go ahead from Jesus. After all, to collect precisely *twelve* baskets of leftovers could hardly seem anything but providential to twelve hungry men, who are by now exhausted and starving.

Does the feeding miracle encourage us to think that Jesus graciously and immediately uses his miraculous powers to come to the aid of his tired and hungry followers? Hardly. It shows us a picture of Jesus whose ability to meet needs is not matched by a burning desire to use it for the benefit of his closest followers. No doubt they finally ate, for the text says that ultimately all were satisfied. But they sure had to wait a long time, and they still did not get the rest they needed!

And then comes the sea-walking episode, or (from the perspective of the disciples) a long night of battling the waves.

It all fits perfectly together. The disciples imagined that the feeding miracle guaranteed them their master's miracle-working power whenever they had a need. But that was a misunderstanding. Jesus has the power to work miraculously, but he does not exercise it freely and immediately whenever life presents discomforts, challenges or dangers. That lesson the disciples had not yet learned. No wonder they misunderstood the sea-crossing episode. It was designed to teach the same lesson! They did not have eyes to see, or ears to hear (cf. 8:17-21).

Not long afterward, Jesus will feed another large crowd (8:1-10). And he will again use a sea-crossing episode to urge his disciples to look more deeply into the meaning of his miracles and the significance of his presence with them (8:14-21; see the next chapter of this book.) It is comforting to know that Jesus does not give up on us when we have trouble understanding. And it is even more comforting to know that when we battle the storms of life, wondering whether Jesus knows or cares, we can be assured that our intercessor is praying for us, praying that our courage, and strength and faith will withstand the storm. And sometimes, if we have eyes to see and ears to hear, we will catch glimpses of Yahweh, as God graciously grants us a glimpse of the divine presence passing by in front of us, and the echoes of God's voice whispering above the roaring of the storm: "I AM! I am with you always!"

Three Lessons from a Boat

Selections from Mark 4, 6 and 8

Three times in Mark, Jesus explicitly predicts that he will be rejected, killed and in three days rise again (8:31; 9:31; 10:33,34). Three times in Gethsemane, Jesus tells his disciples to "watch and pray." Three times, he returns from his own prayer to find them sleeping (14:32-42). Three times, Peter denies his Lord, just as Jesus had predicted (14:68-71; cf. 14:30).

Not a few Markan interpreters have pointed out Mark's penchant for reporting "threefoldedness." But the threefold pattern that has provoked the most interesting and varied discussion involves the three main "boat trips" in Mark's Gospel (4:35-41; 6:45-52; 8:14-21). Other boat trips are alluded to in Mark, but these three stand out as unique. They are reported in greatest detail; they all involve some sort of crisis and Jesus' response; they all report a significant dialogue between Jesus and his disciples; and they all show that the disciples are having a hard time understanding who Jesus is and what he is up to. "Who then is this?" ask the disciples at the end of the first episode (4:41). "They were utterly astounded, for they did not understand ..." comments the narrator at the end of the second trip (6:51,52). And the third features nine penetrating questions by Jesus, culminating in a final exasperated, "Do you still not understand?" (8:21). Apparently the disciples, the narrator and Jesus himself agree on one thing: insight doesn't come easy!

Commentators seem to share that sentiment as they struggle to discern some sort of pattern in the three boat crossings. Some see in them a pattern that focuses on the identity of Jesus. In the first one Jesus authoritatively calms a storm, provoking the disciples to ask,

"Who is this?" (4:41). In the second, while walking on the sea, Jesus calmly identifies himself, saying, "It is I;" or if one looks more carefully in the original language, "I Am" (6:50). In the third (as some interpret the text) Jesus identifies himself symbolically as the "one loaf" which through his death they will share.

Others find a quite different pattern in the three boat crossings. By stilling the storm Jesus symbolically smoothes a path that will eventually connect Jew and Gentile, who lived on opposite sides of the Galilean Sea (4:35-41). By walking on the water and urging the disciples to understand the feeding miracle Jesus has just performed, he prepares to bring Jews and Gentiles together (6:45-52). Finally, in his own body (the *one* loaf in 8:14) he symbolizes the union of Jews and Gentiles as he urges his followers to recognize that the feedings prefigure the salvation of the whole world (8:14-21). And so, to the Christological pattern suggested above, a missionary pattern is added.

My own view is that another pattern shines through when each incident is carefully examined.

Boat trip number one (4:35-41)

Jesus has just taught his disciples that a "secret Kingdom" (4:11) is advancing inexorably toward its final goal. It may begin as vulnerable as seeds thrown on a path, on rocks, among thorns (4:1-20); it may be hidden now (4:21-22); its beginnings may be as small as a mustard seed (4:30-32) and its growth as mysterious as growing crops (4:26,27). But nothing can prevent the great future harvest, the light from shining, the mustard shrub from providing shade and shelter. The Kingdom will succeed, no matter what setbacks there might be along the way. And in case the disciples should have missed the intended meanings, Jesus explained the parables to them in private (4:33,34). The disciples ought to have been ready to face anything! Instead, the very next crisis provokes panic.

The disciples' boat becomes a classroom as Jesus begins to teach his followers that there is no need to fear if Jesus is with them in the boat. A life-threatening storm arises. Jesus sleeps peacefully, fully confident in God's providential care (cf. Ps. 4:8); the disciples, in panic, fight the waves and in desperation wake Jesus with the accusation that he doesn't care about their plight. Do they expect him to join them pulling ropes, or pick up a pail and bail water? Perhaps "pray to his God" (as Jonah's companions in a similar situation woke him to do; cf. Jon. 1:6)? It is hard to imagine that they expect him to calm the sea for them, or they will be less astonished when eventually he does so!

Jesus *rebukes* and *silences* the raging storm. The words remind us of his mastery over demonic powers. Jesus has a much harder time calming the disciples. Even after the storm is stilled they are filled with fear (not awe as NRSV proposes). They have just experienced the unimaginable. Only God can calm a storm at sea (cf. Ps. 107:23-29; 89:9). *"Who is this?"* they ask each other.

The first lesson is over. Jesus has left them with an unanswered question at the end of his teaching session. Readers of Mark's Gospel have an advantage over the uncomprehending disciples. They have been told already in the first verse of Mark's Gospel what Jesus' disciples are struggling to discover: Jesus is the Messiah, God's Son. And through this episode they learn that he is also master of the sea, master of *everything* that threatens our security, and our confidence that the secret Kingdom is truly on its way. Jesus has been granted authority and power to rise up, calm storms, calm us. Why then should we fear?

Boat trip number two (6:45-52)

Though Jesus has the authority and power, that is no guarantee that he will use it every time we face a crisis. This is the lesson the disciples should have learned in lesson number two of their sea-crossing curriculum. The previous chapter in this collection showed that the mysterious meaning of the first feeding miracle (6:30-44) and the hidden clues in the sea-walking episode (6:45-52) reveal a miracle-worker who sometimes has other plans than an immediate rescue. Sometimes we will battle the waves while Jesus prays for us. Sometimes his loving care will be revealed, not in an amazing rescue, but in glimpses of his presence, whispers of his willingness to join us in the storms of life and to accompany us through them.

If lesson one was "Jesus has the power," then lesson two is "... but that does not mean he will immediately remove every obstacle we face!"

Then comes lesson three, and here we must do some detective work with the text (as we did in the previous chapter). There is a hidden meaning here (Mark says so in 8:21), and the reader is challenged to find it.

Boat trip number three (8:14-21)

The text unit is neatly bounded by Jesus' and the disciples' departure from Dalmanutha and arrival at Bethsaida (8:13,22). The episode therefore takes place in the privacy of a boat on the Sea of Galilee. There is no one present to observe the disciples' embarrassment except themselves and Jesus. And embarrassed they must be, for Jesus asks nine consecutive questions, all designed to provoke the disciples to reflect a bit more carefully on the meaning of loaves and leaven, feedings and requests for signs. All the disciples can come up with are two one-word answers, revealing that they remember the details of the feedings, but have no clue what they were to have learned from it all.

It is a puzzling text which scholars have interpreted in an astonishing number of ways. In my opinion, the text makes most sense if it is interpreted along the following lines.

First, the disciples have carelessly begun their journey (presumably around mealtime) without making adequate preparations. A single loaf (in those days the size of a dinner roll) would never do for thirteen travelers (v.14).

Second, Jesus warns them against something that the Pharisees and Herod are doing wrong (v. 15). In keeping with the imagery of the text, he calls it leaven. Since Mark has just painted a negative portrait of the "sign-seeking" Pharisees (cf. 8:11-13) and a few chapters earlier of Herod for his fascination with, but unrepentant and uncomprehending response to, miracles (6:14), it seems clear that "leaven" here refers to a wrong attitude to the miraculous. Jesus does not produce miracles on demand!

Third, the disciples miss the point. They presumably think Jesus is chiding them for their failure to bring enough provisions (v.16). Is he chiding them for something else that is probably in the back of their minds? We shall see.

Fourth, Jesus uses a series of questions designed to expose the disciples' persistent misunderstanding. Evidently they have hard hearts, blind eyes and deaf ears (vv. 17,18).

Fifth, Jesus quizzes them about the number of baskets they collected after the feeding miracles. They show that they have perfect memories (cf. v.18) for they can correctly recall that there were twelve baskets collected the first time and seven the second time.

Finally, Jesus asks, "Do you still not understand?"

Are they supposed to decode some secret symbolic meaning in the number of baskets of food left over (perhaps representing Jews and Gentiles)? Many interpreters have thought so, and they might be right.

But I suspect that Mark's primary goal is to help readers pinpoint the disciples' problem – not a failing memory, but rather dull perceptions.

And suddenly it makes sense that Jesus should first warn against sign-seeking and then call for spiritual perception. The disciples' great need was not for more miracles but for more understanding. Jesus' second lesson in this boat already focused on the fact that miracles may not be granted just because we are experiencing some difficulty. Now Jesus wants his disciples (and Mark wants his readers) to realize that Jesus will not produce miracles on demand, just because someone has a hankering for displays of supernatural power. Jesus categorically refuses to produce them for the Pharisees. And he warns his disciples against their "leaven," calling on them rather to have "hearing ears" and "seeing eyes."

But Jesus' challenge is softened by a promise. If the disciples have deaf ears and blind eyes, the good news is that Jesus can heal both. Mark structures this part of his Gospel like this:

A 7:31-37 Jesus Heals Deaf Ears
  B 8:1-10 The Feeding Miracle
    C 8:11-13 Pharisees Seek Signs
    C' 8:14-15 Disciples Warned Against Seeking Signs
  B' 8:16-21 Disciples Called to Understand Feeding Miracles
A' 8:22-26 Jesus Heals Blind Eyes

Jesus literally "surrounds" his struggling disciples with hints that he can heal deaf ears and blind eyes. In fact, the good news is made even more specific by the nature of the miracle that closes this section. Jesus can even give a second touch to those who can see, but without understanding, like the man who could see people as trees; like the disciples who had the facts of the feeding miracles perfectly memorized, but had failed to understand the significance; like Peter who, in the very next text, correctly identifies Jesus as the Messiah (8:29) and then immediately reveals that he doesn't know what that really means (8:32).

But one question was left hanging earlier. What is going on in the minds of the disciples when Jesus, seemingly out of the blue, warns them against the yeast of the Pharisees? Let's reconstruct the situation.

Last time they were in the boat they had been left hungry all day before the miraculous feeding came. They had been rowing all night before Jesus came to them on the lake. Miracles will not always occur as soon as we sense a need (they were supposed to learn). But they missed the point of it all.

In the meantime Jesus fed another crowd, but this time made them wait three days for the miraculous feeding. Still the meaning escapes them. If their faith can't last three days without a divine miracle, how will they ever be ready for the Passion? In fact, they won't!

After the first feeding, Jesus stooped to the weakness of his disciples. He intended to pass by them, to reveal himself as the presence of God, the one who knows and cares about their struggles, and who will accompany them in their times of storm. But in the end he entered their boat and calms their sea.

After the second feeding, Jesus will not stoop to their weakness. As they cross the sea, shortly after the second feeding miracle, they find themselves with only one loaf in the boat, a perfect situation for a picnic lunch while rowing across Lake Galilee – if only they had remembered to bring along enough food.

Can you picture the scene? They look at their solitary loaf, look at each other, then slowly turn their eyes toward their miracle-working companion. One loaf – no problem! There is someone in the boat who can easily feed them all with this one little loaf. And so someone picks up that one loaf, sidles up to Jesus and with a suggestive gesture says, "Well Lord, we're hungry. Come on, we know you can do it!"

They had failed to understand the feedings. They imagined that somehow the miracles provided a guarantee that Jesus would be there to hand out the miracles whenever they sensed a need. They had missed the point. This time Jesus would not stoop to their weakness. On the contrary, his immediate response is, "Watch out! Watch out for the yeast of the Pharisees and Herod." Watch out for an attitude that thinks signs and wonders are available on demand. Watch out for the blindness that misunderstands the real meaning of God's working. Watch out for the hardness of heart that can be amazed at works of power, but unprepared for the times when the miracles will not be handed out freely.

The usual interpretation of Mark 8:14-21 is very different. Interpreters usually imagine that the disciples are fretting over their lack of provisions and that Jesus is here chiding them for not reckoning with his miracle-working power. They imagine Jesus is saying to his disciples, "If only you had understood the feedings, you would stop fretting about your one little loaf. You'd hand it to me in faith and I'd multiply it before your eyes!"

If we take seriously the way Mark has recorded the whole series of incidents surrounding this text, it looks like the text means virtually the opposite! The seemingly insignificant details in the feeding miracles, the subtleties in the sea-walking episode, the warning against the yeast of the Pharisees and Herod, and the structure of the whole Markan teaching unit – these all conspire to turn the usual reading of Mark 8:14-21 on its head.

The disciples do not fail to realize that Jesus could work miracles. On the contrary, they fail to realize that he will not do it every time they want him to. Of course Jesus *could* multiply their loaf. But if they expect him to jump every time they are hungry or tired, they will never be ready for what lies ahead.

And so lesson three is taught: Jesus will not work miracles on demand, neither to satisfy our lust for supernatural signs, nor to turn life into a picnic.

Putting it all together

The three boat crossings, the two feedings, the larger context of Mark's Gospel all contribute to a fascinating and important portrait of the miracle-working Jesus. His power and authority extend over land and sea, over natural and supernatural enemies. Jesus can miraculously meet needs, but will never produce miracles on demand. He knows our needs, prays for us, passes by, reveals himself as "I Am," "God with us," and calls on us to trust and not be afraid, to be faithful and serve, in good times and in tough times. We are not to seek unambiguous signs, but rather to have hearing ears and seeing eyes, that we might recognize God present and at work among us, come what may.

Mark's Gospel teaches that the way of following Jesus is not always paved with success, glory or comfort. More often it involves suffering, deprivation, rejection, even death – and beyond it, glory! The reign of God will be victorious, but it will seem to suffer setbacks along the way. Jesus teaches those lessons not only when he leads his disciples on the long journey to Jerusalem and the cross, but already on the Sea of Galilee when the disciples' boat becomes his classroom.

Breaking Down Barriers

Mark 7:24-30

Jesus left that place and went to the vicinity of Tyre. He entered a house and did not want anyone to know it; yet he could not keep his presence secret.

In fact, as soon as she heard about him, a woman whose little daughter was possessed by an evil spirit came and fell at his feet. The woman was a Greek, born in Syrian Phoenicia. She begged Jesus to drive the demon out of her daughter.

"First let the children eat all they want," he told her, "for it is not right to take the children's bread and toss it to their dogs."

"Yes, Lord," she replied, "but even the dogs under the table eat the children's crumbs."

Then he told her, "For such a reply you may go; the demon has left your daughter."

She went home and found her child lying on the bed, and the demon gone.

Is it always a sin to be exasperated? I guess I used to think so. Over the years I've become more realistic. It helps to be married and have six children, to have a job that can sometimes be stressful, to discover that not everything in life turns out as one hopes and expects.

Sometimes I am exasperated and I hope it isn't always sin. What does that have to do with this text? Well, I suspect that Jesus was just a bit exasperated. He had just been working with his sometimes dull-minded disciples. They just didn't catch on; they had eyes that didn't see and ears that didn't hear. And just before this incident he had a heated confrontation with legalistic, tradition-bound, hypocritical scribes and Pharisees whose attitudes drew out some *very harsh* words from Jesus.

To get away from the pressure he takes a trip to the coast. His goal is to have a break, to get some rest, to get back his energy and maybe his composure. No sooner does he find a place that he thinks is "far from the maddening crowds," when a woman interrupts his solitude. I think Jesus might be just a bit exasperated when he says, "First let the children eat all they want ... for it is not right to take the children's bread and toss it to their dogs."

But by the time the incident ends, Jesus has poured out grace on a most unlikely candidate. And she, in the process, by her sharp mind and gracious spirit, likely charms a frustrated Jesus. I think they both go on their way with renewed energy and joy and a renewed conviction that God is good and life is too, sometimes. Both see walls come down.

To reach such a conclusion, it is essential to understand what goes on in the dialogue that opens Mark chapter 7. The Pharisees and scribes come and confront Jesus. They are indignant that Jesus' disciples are disregarding the laws governing ceremonial cleansings. The disciples have come from the market place and have proceeded to eat with ceremonially unclean hands. They have flouted the traditions of the elders; they have risked their ritual purity.

The Pharisees care little about dust on hands. I doubt they would have cared if the disciples got food poisoning from contaminating their own food. What matters is that scribal traditions are being ignored. The rules are being broken. And Jesus isn't doing anything about it.

I suppose they hope that by confronting Jesus, they will provoke him to straighten out his disciples. How wrong they are! What Jesus does is turn on the scribes and Pharisees. He cares little about the cleanliness of his disciples' hands. What matters to him is the filth in the Pharisees' hearts!

After the heated confrontation in which Jesus sarcastically informs his enemies that they do a beautiful job of fulfilling the Old Testament – that is, those texts that describe hypocrites! – Jesus turns to the crowds and his disciples, explaining that what really matters is not tradition and ceremonies, religious scruples and legalistic compliance. What really matters is a pure heart.

And then comes the text about the Syrophoenician woman.

By putting these two texts in sequence, Mark has hinted that the real issue is the breaking down of walls. You see, all those rules and regulations, the cultural and religious traditions, played an important function for the scribes and Pharisees. They served to help define right and wrong, pious and profane. They helped separate righteous and sinners, those deserving and those not deserving God's favor. The great walls of tradition and ceremony kept religious leaders walled off from the ordinary Jew and, even more importantly, Jews walled off from their pagan neighbors.

Jesus came to break down walls. He did it by redefining purity as a matter of the heart. In effect, Jesus declared all food clean – especially food eaten with grateful hearts, even if by unclean hands. And he did it by ministering God's grace to people on the "wrong" side of the dividing walls.

In effect, Jesus was saying, "Those walls of tradition and ceremony must come down." Jesus came to break down all the walls that keep people apart – especially those that keep people from the grace of God. He interacted with those whom others called unclean, he associated with those others called sinners, he conversed with Samaritans and Gentiles, *he broke the cherished rules of his religious culture*. And Mark uses chapter 7 of his Gospel to challenge the church to learn from Jesus.

In Mark 7 Jesus meets his match. But it doesn't happen when a powerful coalition of Pharisees and scribes tries to get him. It happens when a witty Greek woman simply will not take "No!" for an answer. If Jesus was at work from the Jewish side, chopping at the foundations of the wall between Jews and Gentiles, this faith-filled woman stood on the other side, waiting for a crack to open up. When it did she pushed her way through. And as she stood before Jesus, he ministered to her – and she to him.

Let's look at this exchange.

Jesus travels northwest toward the coastal city of Tyre, a region far more Gentile than Jewish. Jesus is escaping from the routine of ministry, attempting to get away for much-needed rest. We assume the disciples are with him. As I suggested before, he is probably just a bit exasperated with the narrow-minded religious leaders and the sometimes slow-minded disciples.

But things don't turn out as Jesus anticipated. His reputation as miraculous healer has preceded him, even to the Gentile city of Tyre.

No sooner has he found privacy when a very unlikely candidate for his ministry comes to the door.

One could say the woman is a "born loser" on three counts. She is female. Social mores of the day discouraged this kind of contact between men and women. She is Greek, a Gentile. That puts her on the wrong side of the great barrier – for Jews, at any rate. She is of Syrophoenician origin. This identifies her by race and by religion. The title links her with the Old Testament Canaanites and associates her with the religion of the wicked queen Jezebel. The woman comes to request that Jesus drive a demon from her daughter.

What do you think the scribes and Pharisees would have said about that? I suspect after one glance at her they would have slammed the door and run for the wash basin to cleanse defiled eyes.

Not Jesus. He has just redefined defilement: it is not based on external contacts, but on the condition of the heart. So why does Jesus respond, "First let the children eat all they want, for it is not right to take the children's bread and toss it to their dogs"? Does the confrontation with the religious leaders still have him worked up? Is he impatient that even far from Israel he couldn't get retreat from people clamoring for ministry?

His answer sounds like a snub. It sounds like he's saying, "Sorry. Not now. It's not part of the plan." In fact, it sounds rather like something a Pharisee might say.

> "First let the children eat all they want, for it is not right to take the children's bread and toss it to their dogs."

Is this *Jesus* talking? As we read Mark's text, we wish we could hear Jesus' tone of voice. How serious is he? We wish we could watch his eyes. Are they flashing or are they twinkling? Is Jesus only jesting, testing her faith, perhaps? We don't know for sure, but it's important to hear Jesus' response to her carefully.

He says, "*First* let the children eat." That implies there will be a second. And that, in turn, is a veiled hint that if the request is not granted at this time, it will not be because the person in front of him is a woman, or because she is a Greek, or because she is pagan. A refusal will have nothing to do with gender, ritual uncleanness, racism or even religion. It will be because the right *time* has not yet come. Jesus is doing the things that have to be done first. He is renewing Israel. The time when Christ will remove distinctions between slave and free, Jew and Greek, male and female *is yet to come*.

Another point to notice: The Greek word translated "dogs" is a diminutive. In grammar it is technically a "caritative," something we colloquially call "an endearment term." Jesus does not actually say "dogs;" he says "puppies" (in Greek it is *kunarion*, not *kuōn*). One could even translate it "dear little puppies". In any case the word clearly refers to household pets, not the wild dogs roaming the streets. Furthermore, Jesus doesn't actually call her a dog/puppy. The term is used only as part of an analogy.

Jesus' refusal sounds much different taking this into account. But it's still a refusal – until the woman changes Jesus' mind.

Unfortunately, we also cannot hear the tone of *her* voice or watch the twinkle in *her* eye. But she clearly chooses her words with care. Her first word to Jesus is *nai*. Some translations leave it out, but it is the ordinary Greek word for "yes." "Yes, Lord! Yes, I know that we Gentiles have no place at the table. (Not yet, at any rate.) Yes, I know that the Messiah's mission is to the Jews. Yes, Jesus, what you say is right. I accept it."

Her second word to Jesus is *kurie*. Some translations give the English word "Sir." Now, even if she means to say no more than a polite "Sir" to him, even that would be remarkable in light of Jesus' words to her. But *kurie* can also be translated "Lord." I think this woman is confessing an insight into who this Jesus is, and she is willing to submit herself to him, to call him *Lord*. (Interestingly, the only person in Mark who confesses that Jesus is *Son of God* is also a Gentile; cf. 15:39.)

The woman's third word to Jesus is a very important little word: *kai* – a word that can be translated "and" or "even" or "but." Here it is probably best translated "and yet." The woman is saying, "That is all fine and good. I accept all that about Jewish priority. *And yet*, remember that I was not asking for a seat at the table. I would gladly accept just a small crumb that inadvertently falls while the children are enjoying their feast; that will surely be enough!"

This woman does not cringe at being compared to a puppy. She seizes the designation and uses it to make her request irresistible.

What wit! More importantly, what faith! It is enough to make Jesus change his "No" into a "Yes." All the Pharisees and scribes in the world could not have made him change his mind. The genuine faith of a pagan woman succeeds.

And so Jesus announces that the woman's request has been granted. When she arrives home she will find that the demon has left her daughter. Yet as important as the healing would have been to this woman, it is not the primary issue for Mark. This is not a deliverance story; it is a *faith* story, a *grace* story, a *breaking-down-walls* story.

The dialogue has taken center stage and Mark has highlighted the woman herself, her great exercise of faith, and the fact that Jesus crosses a great barrier to a Gentile. Or is it perhaps the woman who breaks through the wall?

The Syrophoenician woman is an incredible example for us. Her example shows us that our walk with God is not ultimately dependent on how successfully we avoid all the faults of Jesus' opponents. Nor is it ultimately dependent on how successfully we avoid all the vices that flow from a defiled and defiling heart. It is dependent on whether we are receptive to the grace of God, poured out on the undeserving, and on a faith that dares to believe such grace will be given.

This needy Gentile woman could never have qualified for God's grace according to the standards of the Pharisees and scribes. The truth is she could never have qualified according to Jesus' standards either. She moves the heart of Jesus by her open heart, her empty hands, and her daring confidence that whatever Jesus gives will be enough. That is faith! That makes walls come tumbling down.

Jesus and this woman demonstrate the insight and humility needed to recognize the walls that divide, and they model the persistence and courage needed to tear them down. When Jesus chided the Pharisees for their pious, religious walls, could he have known his words would so soon be tested? Who knows when the test will come for us?

Eyes that See Again: Bartimaeus

Mark 10:46-52

In this chapter we will look at two translations of Mark 10:46-52.

New International Version

46 Then they came to Jericho. As Jesus and his disciples, together with a large crowd, were leaving the city, a blind man, Bartimaeus (that is, the Son of Timaeus), was sitting by the roadside begging.

47 When he heard that it was Jesus of Nazareth, he began to shout, "Jesus, Son of David, have mercy on me!"

48 Many rebuked him and told him to be quiet, but he shouted all the more, "Son of David, have mercy on me!"

49 Jesus stopped and said, "Call him."
So they called to the blind man, "Cheer up! On your feet! He's calling you."

50 Throwing his cloak aside, he jumped to his feet and came to Jesus.

51 "What do you want me to do for you?" Jesus asked him.
The blind man said, "Rabbi, I want to see."

52 "Go," said Jesus, "your faith has healed you." Immediately he received his sight and followed Jesus along the road.

New Revised Standard Version

46 They came to Jericho. As he and his disciples and a large crowd were leaving Jericho, Bartimaeus son of Timaeus, a blind beggar, was sitting by the roadside.

47 When he heard that it was Jesus of Nazareth, he began to shout out and say, "Jesus, Son of David, have mercy on me!"

48 Many sternly ordered him to be quiet, but he cried out even more loudly, "Son of David, have mercy on me!"

49 Jesus stood still and said, "Call him here." And they called the blind man, saying to him, "Take heart; get up, he is calling you."

50 So throwing off his cloak, he sprang up and came to Jesus.

51 Then Jesus said to him, "What do you want me to do for you?" The blind man said to him, "My teacher, let me see again."

52 Jesus said to him, "Go; your faith has made you well." Immediately he regained his sight and followed him on the way.

Two versions of a very simple story: One day Jesus passes the spot where a blind man sits begging. The man's calls for mercy attract Jesus' attention. Jesus calls the blind man, asks what he desires, and responds by healing him. Everyone leaves, and the story is over. That's it!

Of course, the careful reader will protest: "There's more to the story than that! People are named, places are identified, there's some fairly dramatic action, even some conflict and a final resolution." True enough. So let's look at some of those details.

Mark has supplied some names for us. The blind man is "Bartimaeus son of Timaeus" (NRSV) or "Bartimaeus (that is, the Son of Timaeus)" (NIV). Let's assume for a minute that these are appropriate translations of what Mark wrote. What would it seem the author is doing? There are three possibilities:

1. Mark might be supplying the names of two men: first the name of the blind beggar (Bartimaeus), then the name of his father (Timaeus). This is the interpretation suggested by the NRSV translation. But that would be of little interest to the reader, since no other information is available anywhere about either of these men.

2. Or, Mark might be telling us only the *blind man's* name (Bartimaeus). However, since his readers do not understand Aramaic, he translates the Aramaic part of the name (bar), explaining to the readers that it means "son." On this reading, we don't know whether the father's name is Timaeus at all (just

as the name "Harrison" means "Son of Harris," even for those who have a father with a different name). The NIV translation would suggest that this was the author's intent. But why should we care what the blind man's name means, and in particular what the Aramaic word "bar" means?

3. A third possibility is that Mark is telling us only the name of the *man's father*. His father's name was "Timaeus." He himself is left unnamed in the text, and perhaps is generally known only as "bar" (i.e. "son of") Timaeus. On this view, one might suspect that his namelessness in the text reflects his low status as a blind beggar.

We're left guessing, wondering why it was important for Mark to waste space on names we hardly care about, and scarcely understand.

We might even puzzle about all the titles used for *Jesus* in this text: Jesus of Nazareth, Son of David, Rabbi (or My Teacher), etc. Why all these titles? What do they all mean?

Our more careful reading would reveal other historical facts, though we would still wonder why they are important. We'd learn that there is a large group of travelers – Jesus, his disciples, and many others. We'd learn that they have just passed through Jericho and are now leaving the city. We'd learn that the beggar is seated until Jesus calls him. We'd get the impression from the NRSV that he has been wearing a cloak (though this is less clear in the NIV), and that he runs to Jesus without it. We'd learn that Bartimaeus joins the troupe after regaining his sight.

A more careful examination of the historical facts uncovers a story with interesting contours . . . and with enough unclarity to raise some questions. But it does little to teach us anything we wouldn't already know by skimming the story. We could, of course, track down similar narratives in Matthew 20:29-34 and Luke 18:35-43 in the hopes that they might help fill out the picture. But that would just leave us with more questions about who got the facts straight, and whether these other stories are actually attempts to supplement Mark's sparse narrative.

So is that all there is here? No indeed. Mark is not merely a historian. Mark is a literary genius and a profound theological thinker. There are buried treasures scattered throughout his Gospel, just waiting to be uncovered! And so we do a double take. This is a story about opening eyes, and not only Bartimaeus is in need of that. Mark, in the subtle and magnificent way he narrates this event, gradually draws the reader also into a new experience of seeing clearly and learning to follow Jesus.

Three themes

Let's start by examining some of the story's features that require only a little digging to reveal their treasures:

First, the matter of faith. Bartimaeus expresses his faith each time he calls out "Have mercy on me!" It is a line he's used a thousand times a day, urging passersby to drop him a coin. Now he utters the line with new meaning and urgency. This time Jesus, the healer, the miracle worker, is passing by. If only Jesus would have mercy on Bartimaeus, would heal his eyes, he'd never have to beg for spare change again.

Bartimaeus' faith seems all the more impressive when we note its persistence. Throughout Mark, faith is marked by concerted efforts to break through barriers. We think of those four bold villagers who, undeterred by massive crowds, tore open a roof and lowered their crippled friend on ropes to Jesus. We think of the unclean woman who pushed her way through the crowd to touch Jesus' garment. We think of the synagogue ruler to whom Jesus said, "Do not fear, only believe," even after death took from him the daughter whom he had asked Jesus to heal. We think of a Gentile woman, courageous enough to challenge even Jesus' own initial refusal with her remarkable comment: "Even the dogs under the table eat the children's crumbs!" Here, Bartimaeus ignores the rebuking crowd, turns up the volume and cries for mercy until Jesus hears and responds. That's faith!

Second, the discipleship journey. This journey through Jericho actually began way back in Mark 8:27, way up north in Caesarea Philippi. The goal of the journey is Jerusalem. A glance ahead in Mark's narrative reveals that the Bartimaeus story is the last event before Jesus enters Jerusalem and continues the journey to the cross—and beyond the cross to glory. Mark's code word for this journey is "on the way." This phrase opens the narrative ("*On the way* he asked them . . ." 8:27) and this phrase ends the narrative (" . . . and followed him *on the way*" 10:52). Moreover, Mark repeatedly uses this phrase to set the pace of the narrative, reminding the readers that Jesus and his disciples are still on their journey, a journey with Jesus leading and the disciples following (or *learning* to follow . . . or more often *not* learning to follow). In fact,

Mark uses the entire journey section to teach the reader, as Jesus was teaching the disciples, what it means to truly follow Jesus, to "set one's mind on divine things, not human things" (see 8:33). As we will see, it is not insignificant that the healed beggar follows Jesus on this journey of discipleship.

Third, the theme of "seeing." Over and over again, Mark highlights the need for "seeing eyes" (cf. 4:12; 8:18). It is not enough to gather data, to remember facts, or to observe what is obvious to the naked eye. The goal is perception, insight, understanding. And so the first half of Mark's Gospel ends with the story of a blind man healed, but healed in two stages. First he "sees" (but cannot distinguish men from trees!), and then he sees "clearly." It requires a second touch from Jesus. And Mark uses this text (8:22-26) as a "hinge transition." It closes the first half of the Gospel, a block of material filled with miracles that the disciples saw but did not understand. And it opens the door to the second half of the gospel, with its discipleship journey. On that journey Jesus will try over and over again to open the disciples' eyes to the true meaning of following Jesus. Unfortunately they will arrive in Jerusalem still half blind, and when they finally see what the road truly entails they will be unwilling to follow. Now Mark closes this highly symbolic "journey to Jerusalem" with another healing account, but not of a man who needs a second touch to see clearly. This is instead a story of a man whose full healing leads to genuine following on the road to the cross. It is a picture of what still needs to happen to the disciples within the narrative – and to the readers of the text.

Faith, following, seeing: these major Markan themes are illuminated by the Bartimaeus text and illustrated by its protagonist. And so the text begins to reveal its depth and speak its words of encouragement and challenge.

Greater depths

Yet this text, perhaps more than most, seems to have *unlimited* depths. One keeps digging and uncovering more and more. I have already hinted that there are differences in the way words and phrases of the text are translated. I suspect that the differences are there because translators continue to struggle with the depth of this text. Should they present the text just as Mark did? Or should they put things into plain and smooth English for the casual reader?

Take, for example, the cloak! What does Bartimaeus do with his cloak when Jesus calls him? According to the NRSV he "throws it off." According to the NIV he "throws it aside." Some have imagined the blind man was *wearing* his cloak and *throws it off* so that he can run to Jesus. But at this point he is still blind! How fast is he planning to run?

What Bartimaeus is really doing with his cloak is *"leaving it behind."* The only other time the Greek word (apoballo) is used in the New Testament it means "abandon" (Heb. 10:35). He has used his cloak to mark his spot beside the road, and to gather the coins that are tossed into his lap. He is blind, after all, and cannot see the coins that passersby give him. As a fisherman uses a net to gather fish, so Bartimaeus uses his cloak to gather coins. And as soon as the comparison is made, the significance of the text also emerges. The first disciples abandoned their nets to follow Jesus – they abandoned their identity, their security, and their livelihood. Jesus was calling them and they were ready to begin a new life of following. Bartimaeus does the same thing. Just as the others left all they had, so does he. No longer will he need to mark his spot beside the road. No longer will he need his cloak to gather coins. He is about to be healed. He is about to become a Jesus follower.

Suddenly we realize that this is not only a *healing* narrative with a focus on Jesus' mercy and power. It is also a *call* narrative! Jesus is *calling* to the blind man and he *leaves everything* to follow Jesus – just as the other disciples had done. And suddenly we marvel again at the quality of Bartimaeus' faith. Not only does he call out over and over again, persisting even in the face of the crowd's opposition. At the call of Jesus, he abandons his old life of begging. And he does it *while he is still blind!* He trusts Jesus to give him a new vocation as a Jesus follower.

And now we must come back to the names! Earlier I quoted two translations showing that in different ways they identify Bartimaeus as "son of Timaeus" – and then leave us unsure about whose name is being supplied: the beggar's, or his father's, or both. But the Greek text behind this translation actually says something else. The man is identified as "Son of Timaeus, Bartimaeus." The names (or titles) are presented the other way around. Hardly any English translation ever preserves the original order, no doubt because it seems like the wrong way to present the information. Why first translate the word "bar" for the reader, and then tell them what the man's name is? It almost seems like Mark is writing in perfectly clear Greek for his reader (and our translations do it for us in English) and then he translates what he has just said into Aramaic. For whom? It all seems incomprehensible until we take something else into account. Not only "bar" has a meaning that we, like the original readers, need translated. "Timaeus" is a name that needs translation, too! Mark does not need to translate it for his readers, because it's a Greek name they already understand. So what does it mean? It means "honor." The fact that Mark puts the title first and then the name strongly suggests that his focus is on the meaning of the title, more than on the *name* of the person.

Let me paraphrase Mark 10:46 this way:

> They came to Jericho. As he and his disciples and a large crowd were leaving Jericho, there beside the road was a son of honor, blind and begging! And guess what? That was his name as well – Son of Honor (Bartimaeus).

In narrating the event, Mark has highlighted the tremendous hiatus between the man's true identity, perhaps his destiny, and his present station in life. He is a "son of honor" – but here he sits blind and begging. Some honor that is!

So, why is that important? Well, bear with me. We come now to Jesus' titles. How does Bartimaeus address Jesus? Both the NIV and the NRSV word it like this: "Jesus, Son of David." And both get it the wrong way around again! I have an eight-translation parallel New Testament. Only the Message preserves the word order that Mark used: "Son of David, Jesus." But why first ascribe the title, then identify the person? Elsewhere in Scripture it is always the other way around. No doubt Mark reverses it here (again!) to highlight the title and its meaning. It is a messianic confession: Jesus is the coming king! Amazingly, the two main characters in this story are identified in rather parallel ways: "Son of Timaeus, Bartimaeus" and "Son of David, Jesus." The focus, both times, is on the title and its meaning.

And when we note this, we recognize that blind Bartimaeus can actually see more clearly than the still-half-blind disciples. One of them, their spokesman Peter, had also confessed that Jesus was the Messiah (8:29). But in doing so he was still "seeing without understanding." He was like the blind man Jesus had just healed, who saw "men as trees" walking. Peter was unable to understand the true significance of

Jesus' Messiahship. And so, when Jesus began to speak of the journey to the cross, Peter rebuked the one whom he had just confessed. And throughout the journey, Peter and the others continue to show us that they are still blind to Jesus' intentions, still struggling to understand the meaning of this journey and its destiny.

Bartimaeus, by contrast, confesses Jesus' Messiahship with the title "Son of David," then repeats the title again in the next verse. But most significant of all, when given the opportunity, he follows this Messiah on the road to the cross. He takes up the discipleship journey *on the way*.

As I wrote in my commentary on this text:

> This man, living daily with the shame of his condition, bestows on Jesus titles of honor. Before the narrative is over, we see Bartimaeus, his honor now fully restored, joining Jesus on the way to dishonor and shame. This text is about shame and honor. It suggests that the greatest honor of all is to be allowed to accompany Jesus, no matter where that road will lead. (*Mark* (2001: Herald Press), 253)

And what about Jesus' question to Bartimaeus? Here is Bartimaeus in front of Jesus. He has heard the call of Jesus. He has responded by leaving everything to be with Jesus – just as the other disciples had done. And he is still blind. Now Jesus asks him an odd question: "What do you want me to do for you?" We might imagine it is merely rhetorical. The answer is obvious. He's blind. He wants to get his sight back. And we would be right. But we would have missed the main point.

Let's go back just one incident in Mark's text. Mark 10:35 tells us that two of those who were among the first to be called to follow Jesus approach him with a request. James and John, the sons of Zebedee, are standing before Jesus. They have heard the call of Jesus. They have responded by leaving everything to be with Jesus – just as Bartimaeus will do in the next incident. Jesus asks them a question: "What do you want me to do for you?" There are amazing similarities in these consecutive narratives. The wording of Jesus' question here and of his question to Bartimaeus are identical.

What does the Son of Honor want Jesus to do? He wants to regain his sight in order that he might follow Jesus on the discipleship road.

What do the Sons of Zebedee want? They want positions of *honor*! They want political prestige! They want power! They want glory! They want to sit on the left and the right of Jesus' throne and reap the benefits of reigning with the kind of Messiah they think they are following.

In Mark's narrative, another man will be the true Son of Honor. It will be a blind beggar who exhibits an incredible faith, who reveals incredible insight (even before Jesus heals his blindness), who makes the ultimate sacrifice (leaving all to follow Jesus), who joins Jesus on the road to suffering and shame, and beyond the shame to glory unspeakable. Yes, Bartimaeus is destined for honor. He is destined to find his true identity as a genuine follower of the one who shows us that true honor is found on the road to the cross, and on its continuation through death to glory.

Those disciples who thought there was a shortcut to glory, who thought honor was gained by sidling up to Jesus and requesting favors from a rising political star – well, they could learn a lot from Bartimaeus. As we all can.

Therefore, Keep Watch!

Mark 14:17 - 15:15; 13:32-37

There are several amazing literary patterns in Mark's account of the passion and death of Jesus. They are amazing, that is, once they are discovered. Until then, they remain simply "new treasures" waiting to be found and cherished. The one to which I will draw attention in this chapter was discovered for the first time (to the best of my knowledge) less than a century ago.

Now, of course, there are always those who will be skeptical of any new discoveries.

> "If it is in the text, then surely it has been in plain sight ever since the text was written. Don't claim some kind of superior insight for modern interpreters. 'If it is true it is not new; if it is new it is not true!'"

So respond the skeptics! Yet sometimes it is our preconceptions that keep us from discovering new insights. And the preconceptions that scholars and ordinary Bible readers alike have held about Mark have not always been appropriate or complimentary!

For more than a thousand years, Mark was considered "Matthew's abbreviator" (following one of the opinions expressed by a group of early church Fathers). Mark's Gospel was viewed as an inferior abstract of the more illustrious Gospel of Matthew, an abstract that unfortunately left out most of Matthew's greatest gems.

When the tide of opinion turned several centuries ago (viewing Mark's Gospel as earlier than Matthew's), Mark was considered nothing but a naive compiler of inherited tradition. His Gospel was a simple collection of stories, lacking both literary art and theological depth. In fact, a century ago, William Wrede wrote:

> He [Mark] did not think through from one point in his presentation to the next . . . Not by a single syllable does he indicate that he desires to see two facts brought into connection which he happens to tell one after the other.

The past hundred years of scholarship have proved Wrede to be wrong. Mark has very carefully structured his entire narrative so that often the best indications of a text's deeper meaning are found in subtle clues carefully embedded in the text and in the way texts "cross-reference," shedding light on other texts that precede or follow.

In fact, one of the most persistent ways Mark alludes to the theological meaning and practical applications of the events he records is by placing them in a "meaningful order." An example that is fairly obvious is Mark 15:37-39, the account of Jesus' death and its immediate aftermath:

- Mark 15:37 says that Jesus cried out and died (breathed his last).
- Mark 15:38 tells us the curtain of the temple was torn from top to bottom.
- Mark 15:39 reports the Centurion's confession: "Surely this was the Son of God."

The recording of these three events one after the other is intended to provoke the reader to reflect on the significance of each of the verses in the light of the others. At the *historical* level there is no explicit connection made between the events reported in verses 37 and 38, nor between the events reported in 38 and 39. In other words, Jesus' loud cry did not cause the curtain to split, nor did the splitting of the curtain lead the centurion to make his confession. The *historical* connection is between verses 37 and 39: the Centurion's confession is provoked by "seeing how Jesus died." This makes the reader wonder why Mark recorded the tearing of the curtain between verses 37 and 39.

Though the tearing of the temple curtain is reported as an event that really happened, its significance in the text is not so much *historical* as *theological*. The reader is called to reflect on the causal link between verses 37 and 39, and how these relate theologically to the event recorded in verse 38. Put another way, by reflecting on the meaning of verse 38 in its context between verses 37 and 39, readers are to reflect on the meaning of Jesus' death:

- it is the final sacrifice, making the temple no longer necessary and thus opening the door of salvation to the Gentiles;
- it reveals the face of God to the *whole world* (there is no longer a veil separating them);
- it seals the fate of those who rejected Jesus (their temple will be destroyed), showing that salvation depends on recognizing Jesus, not on Jewish ethnicity;
- it signals the beginning of the mission to the Gentiles (the Centurion represents those who will come to recognize the significance of his death), etc.

One book lists thirty-five possible nuances on the meaning of Mark 15:38 in its literary context. They cannot *all* be right, but surely Mark wants us to reflect on many of them.

We now turn our attention to another subtle pattern in Mark's passion account. This one remained hidden from view as long as readers of Mark doubted his literary skill and theological depth. Fortunately that day is past! In the 1930's and 40's a few interpreters began to suspect that there was a great deal more depth to Mark than readers had often believed. Two of these, E. Lohmeyer and R. H. Lightfoot, drew attention to the pattern presented below. Since then numerous interpreters have recognized it, though I am not convinced that many have recognized its full significance.

My own work on this passage was a turning point for me, convincing me that Mark's Gospel is indeed characterized by a refined literary art, profound theological insights and challenging practical applications.

The pattern emerges gradually as we reflect on the drama of the last night Jesus spent on earth before his crucifixion, a drama which Mark has presented in four distinct scenes, each featuring a startling contrast. Count them.

The curtain opens first to a scene in an upper room. Here we see a contrast between Judas, who would sell his innocent Lord for mere money, and Jesus giving his own life-blood to buy back the guilty (14:17-26).

Scene two takes place in a garden on the Mount of Olives (14:27-52). Here the contrast is between disciples who sleep and their master who watches and prays. As a result, he is ready for "the hour;" they, by contrast, strike with the sword and flee into the night.

Scene three takes place at the high priest's home, where two people are on trial (14:53-72). Jesus stands before the Jewish High Court and there is willing to lose his life (to save it; cf. 8:35), making the confession that leads to his death sentence. Simultaneously in the courtyard below, Peter is on trial before a servant girl. Desperately trying to save his life, he risks losing it by denying his Lord. In contrast to his courageous, truth-speaking Lord, Peter is a coward who lies through his teeth.

Scene four takes place before Pilate (15:1-15). Here Jesus stands in contrast to both rejecters and would-be followers. The whole religious establishment of Israel rejects the King of the Jews in order to preserve the status quo. By contrast, Jesus willingly goes the way of the cross to institute a new way. Though it costs him everything, Jesus continues on the road to the cross; those who had been called to follow on that road have long since abandoned him.

Each scene reports historical events that combine to make up the fateful night. Together they present a profound composite picture of what discipleship really means: self-giving service on behalf of others, prayer and trust in times of testing, faithful confession whatever the cost, nonconformity to this world's systems in obedience to the Father.

Yet these four scenes do more than define disciples. They also combine to demonstrate all the ways in which disciples fail to live up to the ideal: Judas, the three closest disciples, Peter – indeed, all who should have followed, but in the end abandon or reject Jesus. And they combine to say that though every person may fail, Jesus is faithful. Only he gives his life unreservedly for others (scene one); only he submits totally to God's will and casts his life fully into God's hands (scene two); only he lives by the truth he had preached – those who save their lives will lose them; those who lose their lives will save them (scene three). Only he fulfills the call of God to walk the full distance "carrying the cross" and accomplishing God's will (scene four). Those around Jesus act in self-interest, sleep in the crisis, strike out in terror, flee into the night, deny their Lord, and abandon him in his final suffering.

Mark 14 and 15 present more than a report of Jesus' passion. They present lessons in faithful discipleship and glimpses of the one who is faithful where all others fail, whose death will open the door to their salvation.

This much is profound enough, but not particularly new or surprising. Where is that subtle pattern I promised to reveal? Stick with me.

If we look closely, we discover that each of the four scenes covers a three-hour time period. Two of the time indicators are easy to find, though they stand out more clearly in the original language than they do in English.

The first scene opens with the first time indicator, "in the evening" (14:17). The term in Greek is *opsia*. It is a technical term used to denote the first watch of the night as observed by the Roman occupational troops. It covered the time period from 6:00 PM to 9:00 PM.

The fourth scene also opens with a time indicator, "very early" (15:1). The term in Greek is *proi*, denoting the last watch of the night. It covered the time period from 3:00 AM to 6:00 AM.

What about scenes two and three? The time indicators there may not be quite as obvious to the modern reader, but they are there. In Gethsemane, Jesus leaves his disciples three times to pray for one hour (see 14:37,41). The time period would thus be from 9:00 PM to midnight. When he is finished, he announces, "The hour has come." It is the midnight hour, not only on earthly clocks, but also on God's eschatological timetable. "The Hour" was a technical Jewish term for the time of the Lord's activity. And "the midnight hour" was especially significant. At that very hour, long ago in Egypt, God's angel came down to deliver the Israelites. Each year as Passover was celebrated, God's people looked back to that act of deliverance and forward to the one God had promised. Indeed, many Jews believed it would be at midnight during one of the Passover celebrations that God's Messiah would come to deliver Israel again. On this particular Passover celebration, something does happen at midnight. Throughout Jerusalem, disappointed celebrants would make their way home with a resigned, "Maybe next year." But in Gethsemane Jesus makes the great announcement – "The Hour has come!" The time of waiting has ended. God's deliverer has come, not to kill God's enemies, but to die for them. It is the midnight hour (*mesonuktion* in Greek) ... and, incidentally, that is the technical term for the second of the scheduled "watches" of the Roman night.

That's three of the four night watches: "evening" in the upper room; "midnight" in Gethsemane; and later "early" at Pilate's hall. But is there also a time marker for the scene we missed, that third watch where Jesus and Peter are on trial? There is indeed. Perhaps modern urbanites overlook it; rural people probably don't. I live near enough to the edge of town that I sometimes hear a rooster crow in the early morning. So did Peter! It woke him up to what he had done and started him on the road towards repentance. What Mark's first readers would have known was that the term "cock-crow" (*alektorophonia* in Greek), was more than the name of a sound; it was the name of the third watch of the night.

The time indicators are all there, subtle to be sure, but embedded in the text either by direct reference or allusion. And none are without symbolic significance. Truly it was "evening" (a time when things turned dark indeed) as Jesus faced betrayal by one of his own followers. It was "midnight" (the hour of God's intervention and deliverance) as Jesus became the Passover lamb who would die for the people. It was "cock-crow" (a wake-up call) as Peter realized he had denied his Lord. And it was "early/at dawn" (the dawn of something new) when Jesus picked up his cross to face his destiny.

Yet even such symbolic reflections do not capture the significance of the four time references. They also form a pattern, the subtle pattern which "cross-references" with another text in Mark, that each text might shed light on the other. Here's the subtle surprise I promised.

Mark 13 contains Jesus' discourse to his disciples on how they should live after Jesus leaves them. It holds out the promise that if they will be faithful disciples and witnesses throughout the times of trouble ahead, they will be reunited with the returning Jesus who will come to gather his people. When will this happen? This cannot be known. But in the meantime, disciples must "watch." Jesus' final ringing challenge is: "Therefore keep watch, because you do not know when" (13:32-37).

But what does it mean to watch? Many have thought it means being on the lookout for signs and calculating God's timetable. Mark, I think, goes out of his way to define it in different terms. He says it means to be a faithful disciple – to model oneself after Jesus. He says it means to make the choices Jesus made throughout the passion night.

How do we know Mark wants us to understand "watch" in these terms? Because his account of the Passion is designed to define discipleship this way. And how do we know that this is what "watch" means? Because Mark drops just enough clues for us to make the connection.

He defines "watching" as that which a doorkeeper is called to do, faithfully standing at his post throughout the long night (cf. 13:34-36). And this is how the text words the challenge: "Therefore keep watch, because you do not know when the owner of the house will come back ... in the *evening* ... or at *midnight* ... or *when the rooster crows* .... or *at dawn*" (13:35).

Mark is writing to a persecuted community, calling them to be faithful to their Lord. They must not betray their Lord as Judas did (scene one – in the *evening*). They must not sleep or strike out or flee in the crisis as the disciples did (scene two – at *midnight*). They must not, out of fear, deny their Lord as Peter did (scene three – *when the rooster crowed*). And they must not hide in the religious establishment like the religious leaders did, nor abandon their master in the end like the disciples (scene four – at *dawn*).

On the contrary, they must follow Jesus in a life of self denial (scene one), prayer and trust in God (scene two), courageous confession before the world (scene three) and nonconformity even at the cost of one's life (scene four). If they will be faithful disciples, they will be ready for the return of their master, in whichever watch of the night he might appear.

On the surface, Mark's passion story is just a vivid story of one man going the lonely road to the cross while those who were called to be his followers fail to live up to their name. On a deeper level, it is a remarkable story of Jesus modeling discipleship, modeling "watching," modeling self-giving, dependence on God, courageous testimony and voluntary cross-bearing. It tells us what happened on one fateful night, but also tells us what ought to happen every night and every day as we await the returning Son of Man.

Living as faithful disciples, living the "cross-life," walking the "cross-road," being faithful in every "watch" of the night – that is what Mark's subtle "cross-reference" linking Mark 13 with the Passion Night is designed to teach.

Questions and Answers,
Signs and Riddles

Jesus' Responses to Questions in Mark

Q. What is the normal function of questions?

A. To get answers!

It is amazing how seldom it actually works out that way in Mark's Gospel, especially when the questions are posed to Jesus. All over Mark's Gospel, Jesus is confronted by questioners – demons, the demon-possessed, religious leaders of various kinds, politicians, individuals, the disciples. One would expect Jesus to seize the opportunity to satisfy people's curiosity and hammer home important lessons. But Jesus surprises us. He surprises us by doing all sorts of things in response to questions ... except answer them!

According to my count there are at least thirty direct questions posed to Jesus in Mark. How does Jesus respond to them? What follows is my assessment, though I am well aware that English translations do not always clearly reflect the claims I am making.

Indirect responses

Four times Jesus comes very close to answering questions, but remains just indirect enough to confront his questioners with a challenge. A good example is found in 9:28,29. Jesus' disciples ask him why they were unable to drive out a demon. In Jesus' response (v.29) he does not tell them why they could not. If his response, "This kind can come out only by prayer," leads them to an inevitable conclusion (their prayer life is deficient), this is a conclusion they will need to draw for themselves. Another example is found in 10:26 where Jesus is in dialogue with the "rich young ruler." The disciples struggle with Jesus' claims and ask, "Who then can be saved?" How does Jesus respond? Not by saying who can and who cannot, but by challenging them to be open to God's enabling power (v.27). For other examples, see 10:10-12 and 15:2.

No answer
Often (about six times) Jesus simply refuses to give any kind of "answer" to those who question him. Sometimes he is silent (as he is before the Sanhedrin in 14:60 and before Pilate in 15:5); sometimes he sharply rebukes his questioners (as he does to the demons in 1:25 and to the Pharisees in 7:5,6 and in 8:12); once he flat out announces to his questioners that he does not plan to answer their question (11:33).

Oblique responses
Several times Jesus responds to a question in an oblique way, indicating how people can find the answers to the questions, but not telling them what those answers are. This happens, for example, when the disciples are informed that there is a betrayer in their midst. When Jesus is asked, "It isn't I, is it?" he responds: "It is one of the twelve." The answer is ambiguous enough that it calls each questioner to examine their own heart and answer their own question (cf. 14:19,20). In 14:12,13 when Jesus is asked a question by his disciples, he tells them which instructions they will need to obey if they want to find out the answer. In 2:16,17 he responds to a question with a proverb; he does the same thing again in 6:2-4. It is as though Jesus is saying: If you want the answer to your question, figure it out!

Counter-questions
More than anything else, Jesus responds to questions with questions of his own.

Q. "Why does this fellow talk like that? Who can forgive sins but God alone?"
A. "Why are you thinking these things? Which is easier... ?" (2:7-9)

Q. "Why don't your disciples fast?"
A. "How can they fast when the bridegroom is with them?" (2:18,19)

Q. "Why are they doing what is unlawful on the Sabbath?"
A. "Have you never read what David did?" (2:24,25)

Q. "Don't you care if we drown?"
A. "Why are you so afraid?" (4:38-40)

Q. "Are we to go and spend that much on bread and give it to them to eat?"
A. "How many loaves do you have?" (6:36,37)

Q. "Is it lawful for a man to divorce his wife?"
A. "What did Moses command you?" (10:2,3)

Q. "Is it right to pay taxes to Caesar or not? Should we pay or shouldn't we?"
A. "Why are you trying to trap me? Whose portrait is this and whose inscription?" (12:14,16)

That's seven examples. According to my count there are at least nine more. And if that is not surprising enough, consider the fact that at least twenty-two additional times, Jesus is confronted with a situation and responds to it with a question. For example: the scribes accuse Jesus of driving out demons in Satan's power. His response – a question: "How can Satan drive out Satan?" (3:22,23). Another example: Jesus is informed that his mother and brothers are seeking him. His response – a question: "Who are my mother and my brothers?" (3:32,33).

In Mark there are far more questions asked than answered. Jesus does not seem overly eager to make sure all questions are answered and neither does Mark. Both seem to put a higher priority on asking probing questions and challenging people to seek insight. When the blind are brought to Jesus, he opens their eyes. When the deaf are brought, he opens their ears. He does not draw pictures for the deaf and describe the landscape to the blind. And it's exactly the same with "spiritual ears" and "spiritual eyes." Jesus is much more interested in opening eyes and ears so that people can hear and see for themselves. He challenges them with riddles and parables, and critiques them for their blindness. What he does not do is tell them precisely what they should be hearing and show them what they should see.

Direct answers

Does Jesus *never* directly answer any questions in Mark? He does, but according to my reading, *only twice!* Yet even here Jesus remains in full control, for both times, after giving a clear and unambiguous answer, he immediately supplements his direct answer with more than the questioner(s) wanted to know.

A scribe wants to know which is the greatest commandment; Jesus tells him, but then immediately adds a second (cf. 12:28-31). The High Priest asks if Jesus is "Christ" and "God's Son;" he says "Yes" to the question, then immediately supplements these two Christological titles with two more of his own (he is also truly divine [*ego eimi*, I Am] and will some day come as the final judge (14:61,62). On these two occasions Jesus gives direct answers, and then gives his questioners more than they bargained for. It is perhaps more than coincidental that direct answers are given precisely when people want to know who Jesus claims to be and when they are prepared to learn from him what God's highest will is. Such questions Jesus is prepared to answer, for when we accept his answers to these questions, our eyes and ears can be opened, enabling us to seek answers to other questions.

What about Mark 13?

The perceptive reader will probably protest that there is at least one other time when Jesus directly answers questions in Mark. In Mark 13:4, in response to his prediction that the temple will be destroyed, Jesus is asked by four disciples, "When will this be, and what will be the sign that all these things are about to be accomplished?" What follows (some would claim) is a very long answer to the disciples' questions. In it Jesus provides a long list of signs and numerous statements designed to help the disciples figure out when "all these things are about to be accomplished."

There are many reasons why I am persuaded that Mark 13 is anything but an answer to the disciples' questions. For one, not a single event in Jesus' long response is called a "sign" . . . indeed the word itself is used only once, to warn the disciples *against* those who give signs! Moreover, Jesus had indicated earlier in his Gospel that "this generation" will not get any signs! (cf. 8:12)

Years ago, during my doctoral studies, I was puzzling over the myriad of different interpretations of Mark 13, noting that some interpreters find in Mark 13 one sign, some many signs, some none at all.

I remember running across a quotation that went something like this: "If the disciples ask Jesus which signs will precede the End of the Age, shouldn't we suppose that whatever follows must be Jesus' answer to the disciples' question?" That is when I decided to check how valid that scholar's assumptions were. After examining more than thirty questions posed to Jesus and more then twenty other situations that promoted a response from Jesus, I discovered that Jesus provides a clear and direct response about four percent of the time. That surely does not provide convincing evidence that if the disciples wanted a sign from Jesus, then he must have granted their request.

Mark 13 is, on the contrary, a sustained attempt by Jesus to redirect the priorities of the disciples *away* from sign-seeking, toward the things that really matter – things like discernment (vv. 5,14a,23,28-31), allegiance to Jesus (v. 6,21,22), courage and obedience in times of trouble (vv. 7,8,14b-17), faithful discipleship (vv. 33-37) even under persecution (vv. 9,11-13), Gospel proclamation (v. 10), prayer and endurance (vv. 18-20,32), and above all, an unfailing confidence that Jesus will someday return to gather his faithful people (vv. 24-27). When *these* are our priorities, then we will not be deceived by those who claim to know more about the timing of Jesus' return than he himself did (cf. 13:32), nor distracted from faithful discipleship by those whose focus is on signs. If our eyes are open only for so-called "Signs of the End Times," Mark 13 will be a permanent riddle. But it will provide the same clear guidance that we find in the rest of Mark's Gospel if what we really want to know from Jesus is:

- Are you the Christ, the Son of God? and
- Of all the commandments, which is the most important?

When these are our priorities, then along with the disciples we will hear the voice that speaks into Mark's Gospel at its very middle, the voice of God saying of Jesus, "This is my Son, the beloved. Listen to him!" (9:7). Mark's Gospel is all about a correct Christology and obedient responses.

Beginning Again

Mark 16:1-8

The footnotes in our Bibles are wonderful – when they help explain something puzzling in the text. But what do we do with the footnotes that puzzle us far more than the texts themselves?

Of all the footnotes to be found in modern translations of the Bible, surely none are more puzzling (perhaps disturbing) than those that comment on the ending of Mark. In the NRSV Bible in front of me, a single footnote suggests no less than *four* different ways in which, according to ancient manuscripts, Mark's Gospel is thought to have ended. "Some of the most ancient authorities bring the book to a close at the end of verse 8." So begins the footnote, alluding to the first option found in the manuscript tradition. Three more options are alluded to when the footnote indicates that some manuscripts end the Gospel with the "shorter ending" and some with the "longer ending" and some with *both*. These "longer" and "shorter" endings are then printed in the main text after 16:8. To complicate things even more, another footnote on the same page indicates that the "longer ending" is lengthened further by an additional four sentences in yet other old manuscripts. If the full story had been told, still other endings would have been included in additional footnotes!

Most of us grew up reading Mark's Gospel as though the verses we call 16:9-20 belonged to the original text. There in the short space of 12 verses we read of three resurrection appearances: to Mary Magdalene; to the two "Emmaus" disciples; and to "the eleven." Not only that; we are also told that the disciples had trouble believing and that Jesus rebuked them for their unbelief. Then comes a form of the Great Commission, a series of promises to the disciples, a report of Jesus' ascension and even a very brief summary of the missionary expansion of the church. All that in twelve verses. It is a breath-taking panoramic survey of everything important from the Resurrection onward. The only problem is: It wasn't written by Mark!

Even conservative scholars have gradually been forced by the evidence to reach this conclusion. And the evidence truly is overwhelming: the earliest commentators on Mark's text make no reference to these verses; the first references made to them are comments that they are *not* authentic; the transition from verse 8 to verses 9-10 is very awkward, reintroducing Mary Magdalene as though she had not been present in the preceding verses, and awkwardly contradicting what Mark wrote in verse 8; verses 9-20 contain both vocabulary and themes that would seem far more at home in Luke than in Mark; finally, not only do *"some* of the most ancient authorities" lack these verses (as NRSV says) – *all* the oldest manuscripts do! And as for the other alternative endings attached to 16:8, they are (if possible) even harder to defend.

But surely Mark's Gospel couldn't possibly end at 16:8! So argue many interpreters. You can't end a Gospel on a note of fearful flight and disobedient silence, especially if not a single resurrection appearance has been narrated. No wonder the ancient Christian scribes tried to give the Gospel a proper ending! And then the speculation begins: perhaps Mark himself wrote a *proper* ending but it somehow got lost; or maybe he *intended* to write more, but was prevented (perhaps by martyrdom) from doing so. I have always been amazed at the eagerness of scholars, especially conservative ones, to grasp at these hypotheses. Do they assume the last verses of Mark weren't as inspired as the rest, so God's Spirit "made them disappear"? Or do they believe that the real ending was as inspired as the rest, but unfortunately God didn't keep it in existence long enough for anyone to know about it? Do they really believe that God chose Mark to write the Gospel, but couldn't keep him alive long enough to finish the job?

Why not simply accept the conclusion best supported by the evidence, namely that Mark's Gospel ends (and was always intended to end) at 16:8? There are two reasons people typically give as to why that can't be done.

First, it is not possible (so it is claimed) to end a Gospel without reporting resurrection appearances! Just look at the other Gospels; all of them feature reports of Jesus' appearances to his followers; obviously,

Mark's Gospel is incomplete without them. That seems like a strange argument to me. None of the Gospels end at the same point as any other. Luke contains a resurrection report, resurrection appearances, a reference to the future worldwide mission, and a report of Jesus' ascension. Of these four events, Matthew includes only the first three, John only the first two, and Mark only the first one. Apparently there are lots of different ways to end a Gospel. Moreover, if Mark wrote first (which is likely), he could hardly have learned from the others what constitutes a "proper" ending. The Gospel story is not told to its very end in any Gospel, not even if we consider Acts to be the continuation of Luke. What gives us the right to tell Mark what he should have included?

Mark knows that the Gospel story includes resurrection appearances (see 14:28), a commission to evangelize (see 13:10), and Jesus' ascension (see 12:10,11,36). He simply chose to refer to these events earlier in the Gospel and not report them at the end.

But there is a second objection, and this is the more serious one. It just doesn't make sense (so it is argued) to say the women were disobediently silent about the resurrection, and then stop there. This is a direct contradiction to what the other Gospels say, and besides, who would think of ending his "good news" like that? This objection must be faced head on if we are going to reach any satisfactory conclusions about the content and meaning of Mark's ending.

As to the supposed contradiction: unfortunately that problem will not go away, *no matter what theory we hold*. Mark 16:8 contradicts Matthew, Luke and John no more and no less than it contradicts every other proposed ending of Mark's Gospel! That means nothing is gained by attaching one of the proposed endings to 16:8. It just imports the problem into Mark's Gospel itself! Everyone, including presumably Mark, must have known that the women *eventually* overcame their fear and reported the good news. But Mark is content to report their (initial) silence. And since every manuscript contains verse 8, everyone has to come to terms with that verse, no matter how they think the Gospel really ended.

Now, there is one easy solution to the problem of 16:8 ... *if only it worked*. Some interpreters have tried courageously to re-read the Greek text and then interpret Mark 16:8 as a description, not of the women's panicky disobedience, but of their awe-inspired obedient haste to do exactly what they had been told to do.

"They went out and fled from the tomb" is then interpreted to mean "they immediately left and in great haste ran to obey." The next line, "for terror and amazement had seized them," is taken to mean "for they were filled with awe and wonder." "They said nothing to anyone" is understood as "they even avoided the normal custom of greeting people along the road," and finally "for they were afraid" is read as "that's how awe-struck they were with the good news." It is a valiant attempt, but unfortunately, it works even less well as an interpretation of the Greek text than of the English. In Mark, "fleeing" (*pheugo*) is virtually a technical term for abandoning discipleship, becoming a deserter (cf. 14:29,50,52) and "fear" (*phobeomai*/ *phobos*) is in fact the enemy of faith (cf. 4:40, 5:36).

So what conclusions have I personally reached about the ending of Mark? Here they are:

- Mark 16:8 is indeed the ending that the author intended.
- It is an ending that combines a great promise with a serious challenge.
- It is a subtle ending, but one perfectly suited to the kind of Gospel Mark wrote.
- It is an ending that "wraps up" Mark's Gospel perfectly, tying up loose ends that Mark has deliberately left dangling along the way.

Now for my interpretation of Mark 16:

Mark's last chapter reports that three women come to Jesus' tomb on Sunday morning, intending to honor him by anointing his corpse. For all their good intentions, they really do get *everything* wrong! First, their timing is wrong – another woman discerned the times and anointed Jesus' body earlier (cf. 14:8). Second, they worry for nothing about a stone too large to move – when they arrive, it has already been rolled away. Third, they respond with fear at what they find inside – and are immediately told that their reaction is wrong. The reader is actually quite well-prepared for their final reaction, their disobedient silence.

A young man (clearly a divine messenger, though Mark does not tell us it is an angel), announces that the crucified one has risen. The women are invited to see where the body had been and then told to report to the disciples that Jesus is waiting to meet them in Galilee. So far, so good. But then the shocking ending: they ran away in fear and remained silent. The reader who has come with them to the tomb is left standing there bewildered: what now? But there is only silence! *What does it mean?*

Sometimes, Mark's Gospel is interpreted as though it was designed to undercut the authority of the first apostles. Mark makes them "look bad" all over the place and then, in the end, denies them a meeting with the risen Jesus. If the women never reported the messenger's announcement, presumably the disciples never went to Galilee. "And that is why you just can't trust those apostles in Jerusalem" (Mark says under his breath). That is how the argument goes. I don't buy it!

Now, of course nobody believes that this is what really happened in *history*. But some scholars seriously interpret *Mark's narrative* that way. Others modify the theory slightly, claiming that Mark is not really discrediting the literal apostles; he is discrediting other church leaders in his own day, first by caricaturing them in the Gospel as the (mostly uncomprehending) disciples of Jesus, and then hinting, at the end, that they've never truly met the resurrected Jesus. I don't buy this theory either.

How Mark could have "loved Jesus and hated the apostles" is beyond me! And that he used the apostles as literary foils for his own theological opponents is a theory for which there is no evidence. Some better solution to the problem of Mark's ending will have to be found. I suggest the following:

First, Mark did not report everything he knew! That is obvious from the fact that the great commission and the ascension of Jesus are alluded to earlier in the narrative. Further, Mark's readers obviously knew enough of their own church history to realize that the women eventually told, and that the followers of Jesus eventually met the resurrected Jesus in Galilee and elsewhere. Our task here is to interpret "the narrative Mark wrote" and not to make a list of all the other things that happened after Easter.

Second, we know that according to Mark, Jesus' followers *did* meet Jesus in Galilee. We learn in 14:27,28 that such a meeting was a prerequisite to future faithfulness and future faithfulness is assumed in texts like 9:9, 10:39 and 13:9-13. Our task is to understand the meaning and challenge of a Gospel ending that does not include a *report* of the Galilean reunion.

Third, we dare not overlook the importance of 14:27,28 in Mark's narrative. There Jesus informs his disciples, even before they abandon him, that there will be a post-resurrection meeting in Galilee. Earlier he had told them when to expect the resurrection (cf. 8:31; 9:31; 10:34). That means the disciples know where and when they are to meet Jesus, whether the women ever tell them or not. The theory that the women's silence is Mark's final *coup de gras* on the male disciples just doesn't work!

Fourth (and here is where things get interesting), the original text of Mark 16:7 can be translated two ways. NIV translates it as a *direct* quote and NRSV as an *indirect* quote – like this:

> Go, tell his disciples and Peter, "He is going ahead of you into Galilee. There you will see him, just as he told you." (NIV)

> Go, tell his disciples and Peter that he is going ahead of you to Galilee; there you will see him, just as he told you. (NRSV)

The difference seems small, until we ask to whom the word "you" refers. According to the NIV it refers to the male disciples. The women are to go tell *them*, "Jesus is going ahead of *you* into Galilee." In the NRSV version "you" includes the women. They are to join the male disciples and tell them, "Jesus is going ahead of *us* to Galilee."

According to the NIV, the women's role is only to be a communication link to the male disciples, telling them what they already know. According to NRSV, they are to join (actually re-join, see below) the male disciples and as a (re)united group travel back to Galilee, meet Jesus and "start over" once again. For reasons that will become obvious, I prefer the NRSV version.

Fifth, we can now see how subtly Mark has woven together two separate stories. First, the story of the male disciples: they follow and serve Jesus in Galilee, then follow him to Jerusalem. There they fail him in the crisis, abandoning him just as Jesus himself is taken away to be tried and crucified (cf. 14:50-72). But just before their final failure they are offered "discipleship-renewal" on the other side of the cross and the resurrection. They are assured that whatever failure intervenes, they can return to Jesus and start over (14:27,28). That is the story of the male disciples; not once prior to Jesus' death does Mark even hint that there were women in the group of Jesus' followers all along.

After Jesus dies, Mark tells the story of the women disciples. We learn now that they too followed and served Jesus in Galilee, then followed him to Jerusalem (cf. 15:40,42). They did not abandon Jesus in the crisis and therefore serve as witnesses to the death (15:40), burial (15:47) and resurrection (16:5,6). In the end, the women also fail (16:8) but not before they too, just like the men, are offered the opportunity to meet the risen Jesus on the other side of failure, to go back to Galilee and "start over" (16:7). Mark reports their failure (16:8), and the narrative is over.

The men failed to stay with Jesus on the road to the cross. The women failed to proclaim the message of the resurrection. Remember why Jesus recruited the disciples in the first place? – "to be *with him*, and to be sent out *to proclaim* the message . . ." (3:14). Mark tells two stories, allowing the male and female disciples (respectively) to represent two ways people can fall short of their calling. Everyone misses the mark, and everyone is invited to start over in the power of the resurrected Jesus. That is Mark's message.

Sixth, Mark now waits for his readers to react!

Some react like this: "Did the women ever join the other disciples? Did they go to meet Jesus in Galilee?" And Mark's Gospel says: "That's *their* story. What matters here is *your* story. You have now heard the message; will you go?"

Others react like this: "Women, how could you? How could you hear the wonderful resurrection message and then be silent?" And Mark's Gospel whispers back, "How can *you*? How can *you* be silent in the face of the same message?" And we realize that just as Nathan "caught" David with a self-condemning parable (cf. 2 Sam. 12:7), Mark's Gospel also "catches" us.

Still others react: "I think I also need to meet the resurrected Jesus in "Galilee." And Mark's Gospel says, "the good news is that *all* are invited to the Galilee reunion – the men, the women, even those who have failed most seriously." That is why Peter is mentioned separately in 16:7 – *even Peter* (as the original should be translated). *All* can meet the resurrected Jesus, indeed all *must* – faithful discipleship depends on it!

And of course there are always those who react: "I would have preferred a different ending, maybe one that rounds it all off nicely and doesn't demand quite as much from me, the reader." How about the "longer ending" that summarizes early church history? Or maybe the "shorter ending" that reads like this:

> And all that had been commanded them they told briefly to those around Peter. And afterward Jesus himself sent out through them, from east to west, the sacred and imperishable proclamation of eternal salvation.

And Mark's Gospel says, "Yes, happy endings are wonderful. The problem is they let us put down the book with a sigh of relief and say, 'Great story!' This is a different kind of book. You cannot put it down, even if you want to. Whether this book has a good or a bad ending depends on you. You are still writing it!" Mark's narrative ends with 16:8, but his story goes on! Mark's Gospel is "The beginning of the good news" (1:1). Our story is its continuation.

Enriching Our Christmas Traditions

Luke 2:1-7

Christmas is a time where traditions become important. We sing traditional Christmas songs. We enjoy the family traditions we have inherited from our childhood or developed in our own families. And we retell the old, old Christmas story that never changes. We read the story, perhaps we recite it, or maybe (as in our family) we act it out.

We relive with Mary and Joseph the long, grueling trip to Bethlehem that was just a bit much for a nine-month-pregnant woman and led to a short labor and delivery on the night of their arrival in Bethlehem.

We respond with astonishment once more that the arriving king is not born in a palace, not even in a house or a hotel room, but in a barn. His first bed is a feeding trough!

We hear the angels' message, run with the shepherds to see, ponder with Mary ... in short, we relive the old story that never changes.

We try to make the traditions come alive and we supplement them with traditions of our own – traditions about trees and gifts and guests and Christmas dinners and lots of things that are designed to make Christmas special, but often make it a dizzying cycle of busy activity and stressed nerves. Right?

Perhaps we have also developed some traditions that don't really enrich our Christmas celebrating. I think about some of those as I reflect on Christmases past. Do you remember last year's celebration? I don't know how your celebration was, but if you will permit me to be a bit tongue-in-cheek, let me describe a typical Christmas.

For months people think about it, worry about it, plan for it, and save for it. Around the beginning of December (or November? or October?), visible evidences of the coming of Christmas begin to appear. Huge advertisements arrive in the malls. Decorations are mounted on light poles. Hubbies complain that they have to risk their lives on the step-ladder again, as they mount strings of lights to the rain gutters. (Why can't their wives do it this year? Equality cuts both ways, doesn't it?)

Christmas trees are sold all over the city and they soon appear in living rooms, all dressed up with tinsel, lights and ornaments. And then it's time to start buying gifts. With that begins the great Christmas competition – competition over who can find parking spots, who can squeeze into already-crowded stores, who can sneak a few places forward in the check-out lines, competition over which store sells the most, which parents buy the most, which children get the most. People stock up on candies, nuts and turkey. Countless hours are spent cooking and baking and working overtime to pay for it all.

As the great day gets closer the pace quickens. People get more tense and touchy. Mom complains about all the banquets that have to be prepared; Dad complains that the family gatherings are getting too huge and expensive; kids complain that they're not allowed to open their gifts on the twenty-third already.

People travel hundreds of miles to fulfill obligations to their families. They come home late, tired and grumpy. People overeat on Christmas turkey; some over-drink on Christmas cheer.

Christmas comes with a big splash, and if we're not careful, that splash washes out our best-laid plans for a nice, quiet, meaningful Christmas.

And then come the after-Christmas blues – you know, exchanging all those gifts that don't fit or were of little value anyway, taking down the decorations, cleaning up the tree, not to mention cleaning up all those new toys that are always lying around, perhaps already broken, on the living room floor.

Slowly Christmas fades away, and everyone breathes a sigh of relief. That was Christmas! Well, maybe not quite. But maybe it's not that far off, either.

So what can we do? Well, we could try to boycott Christmas – just not do all the things that make the season so hectic and often so empty. We could try to live without a tree; after all, there wasn't a decorated tree in the stable, was there? And we could try to live without banquets and feasts; after all, the shepherds were probably eating barley bread and maybe some dried fish on those hillsides. And gifts: well, why not just think of some good gift certificates, pass them around and consider it taken care of? And who needs Christmas cards? We don't really need to visit our relatives, do we? ... Well, I assume you're as skeptical about this solution as I am.

No, if things are going to be different, the difference will need to take place on the inside, not among all the trimmings. A meaningful Christmas will depend far more on our inner attitude than on the external events that mark the season.

I want to make a radical suggestion. I want to suggest that we reexamine Luke's account of Christmas and re-image what took place on that first Christmas night. I don't mean invent a new story. I mean take the Bible very seriously, but fill in the gaps differently than we are accustomed to doing.

Or have you never noticed how much of the Christmas story we actually make up with our own imaginations?

- How many wise men were there? Who knows? The Bible doesn't tell us . . . so we make it three! You know, standardize it, so we can create the right number of figures for the Christmas display.

- And which animals were there in the stable? Who knows? The Bible doesn't tell us . . . so we make it an ox and an ass. You know, "Ox and ass before him bow and he is in the manger now." O yes, the little shepherd boy was carrying a lamb with him, wasn't he? I never could figure out how he carried the lamb and played his little drum at the same time.

- And we use great imagination on the evil innkeeper. He's the bad guy in the story. Whole Sunday school plays center on his opportunism (taking advantage of market conditions to quadruple his rates), his callous blindness (not recognizing the coming of the Lord of Glory), his hard-heartedness (not even finding room for an expecting couple) and his economic chauvinism. Poor carpenters just didn't cut it; you had to be a Roman census official or a respected Jewish leader to find a room in his hotel on that busy night.

And so on and so on. We just fill in the details of the story. We use our imaginations to round out the bare details that Luke and Matthew have supplied. In fact, when we use our imaginations, we often imagine things that we are convinced did not happen. The Bible says the shepherds came to a manger and the wise men came to a house. But it fits better under the tree if we just put them all together.

And even though most people are convinced that the wise men came considerably later (after all, Herod tried to kill all the babies two years and younger and it took a long time to travel from the far east) we just put that star right up there and let it shine on the manger scene on the very first Christmas night.

And having created our images of Bethlehem, we let the story challenge us – challenge us to be as peaceful and calm as the shepherds on the hillside, as filled with worship and praise as the angels, as generous as the wise men, as contemplative as Mary, as obedient as Joseph.

It's a beautiful story, this one we've filled in for ourselves, no matter how probable or improbable our imaginations are – well, beautiful except for that old innkeeper. But we need him as our scapegoat. After all, the larger than life "good guys" in the story leave us with an impossible ideal. One thing comforts us: at least we aren't as bad as the innkeeper!

I suggested before that we re-image the Christmas story – that we imagine it having happened just a little differently than we usually do. I want to suggest a way of re-telling that story. It begins with the question, "How did the innkeeper get into our story?"

Well, we get the idea of the innkeeper from the mention of the inn. "No room in the inn" must mean that some innkeeper didn't make room.

But the story in Luke doesn't actually refer to an inn either – not in the original language at least. When Luke said, "There was no room in the *inn*," he used a word that *could* mean "inn," but almost never does. It almost always means "guestroom."

The word used is *kataluma*, a word used exactly three times in the Bible – once here in Luke 2 where we usually translate it "inn." The other two occurrences are in Luke 22 and Mark 14. In both of those cases, it refers to the room in which Jesus had the Last Supper with his disciples, and they certainly did not go to an inn! They were in a room that is clearly described by Luke as a "large upper room." It is a large guestroom built on the top of a normal house. That is where most Jewish families would build their guestroom, their *kataluma*.

So if the word clearly means "guestroom on top of a house" in two of the three occurrences in the Bible, it's likely that it means this in Luke 2 as well.

Elsewhere in his Gospel, Luke uses a *different* word to refer to an inn. And in that connection he refers to an actual innkeeper. We find this in the parable of the Good Samaritan. The Good Samaritan takes the injured man to an inn – not a guestroom in a house – and the word used is *pandocheion*. He even calls the innkeeper by the corresponding title: the *pandocheus*.

So what does all this mean for our understanding of the Christmas story? Well, taking into account the way Luke uses the words *kataluma* and *pandocheion*, it's likely that in Luke's Christmas story the text actually says, "They laid him in a manger because there was no room for them in the *guestroom*." The baby Jesus was laid in a manger because the guestroom on top of the house was already occupied by other guests!

I can imagine you saying, "Inn, guestroom – what's the difference? They're both places to sleep, and who cares if Joseph and Mary had to go to the barn because the inn was full, or because the guestroom was full? It all comes out the same, doesn't it?"

Well, here is where everything gets interesting. With a closer reading of the text, there is more that disappears from the story than just the inn – and of course with it, the evil innkeeper. There is no stable either.

Check your Bibles. Do they mention a stable? Nope.

"But," we protest, "there *must* have been a stable. There was a manger and a manger means a stable." Not necessarily.

Evidence from all over the Old and New Testaments shows that a typical first-century Palestinian manger was not to be found in a stable, i.e. a separate building made just for animals. It was to be found in the living room of the family's large, one-room split-level house. The typical Palestinian peasant's house was one large room under a flat roof. It was built with two floor levels, an upper level where the family lived, ate and slept, and a lower level where the animals normally spent the night (and then of course there might be a guestroom on the roof!).

So where was the manger? In the most logical place in such a house: built into the floor of the living area, right next to the lower level where the animals were kept. That way the animals could stand in their lower level and eat hay from the manger built into the floor of the higher level.

A typical manger was in the living room of a house. What does *that* do to the Christmas story? Now not only the innkeeper and his inn disappear, but the stable does as well.

When Luke 2 says, "They wrapped the baby in strips of cloth and laid him in a manger, because there was no room for them in the *kataluma*," it isn't saying, "They had to go to the barn because the innkeeper was too hard-hearted to make a room available for the holy couple." Rather it's saying, "They were taken right into the living room, because the guestroom was already full."

The story is not about a full hotel, an evil innkeeper and the cold, dark barn. It is about a typical Palestinian house – one that made room for the holy couple, even though the guestroom was already occupied by other friends or relatives crowding into Bethlehem for the census.

If this way of reading the text is correct, what do we gain, and what do we lose?

Well, this way of reading the story actually saves us a lot of trouble. It actually makes more sense of what we read in the Bible.

We don't have to imagine that Jesus was born on the very night that Mary and Joseph arrived in Bethlehem. The way Luke tells the story, it sounds rather as though she spent the last weeks or months of her pregnancy there. We don't have to wonder how Mary, who has relatives in the hill-country of Judea, and Joseph, who is a native son of the village, can't find a single family (let alone one of their many relatives) who will take them in for the night, or for a week, or perhaps for the last months of Mary's pregnancy. We've had to imagine Mary and Joseph arriving the night of Jesus' birth in order to explain why they couldn't find a decent place to sleep.

With this new reading we are also saved the bother of wondering why the shepherds entered Bethlehem, only to leave the town again to look for a barn.

Best of all, we don't have to invent a new house that the family moved to after Jesus' birth, but before the wise men arrived. After all, if the shepherds came to a manger and the wise men to a house, they must have moved in the meantime – at least the way we usually read the story. But with this new reading, they're in the same house all the time!

And that means there is no trouble believing that the wise men and the shepherds all gathered *together* to worship Jesus – rich and poor, Jew and Gentile – worshiping the one born to be King. And we can even imagine that the star leading the wise men to the place Jesus lay shone over the house not months later, but on that first Christmas night!

And so, instead of re-imaging the story in such a way that we have to throw away all our manger scenes, we actually find a story that makes appropriate even those parts that we thought didn't quite represent what actually happened. After all, there was still a manger and there were still animals, and we could actually argue that this means there really was a stable, even if it was part of the house!

The only thing we really lose is the evil innkeeper – our scapegoat. But then, maybe we can find better motivations for enjoying a meaningful Christmas than staying a couple steps ahead of that old scrooge.

In my opinion, with the new way of reading Luke 2 we gain far more than we lose. We lose our scapegoat, the evil innkeeper. But we gain a wonderful picture of what it really meant for Jesus to come down from heaven to join humanity – a picture of God coming down to identify with common folks like you and me, coming down right where we are, being born in a normal home like all the other babies in Bethlehem. There were probably any number of babies enjoying the soft hay of mangers in the living rooms of other crowded homes in Bethlehem that year.

So what does all this say about *our* Christmas celebrating? I referred to the reliving of the old Christmas story that never changes. Well, its essence never changes, but a little creative imagination might change some of the ways we think about it.

If our Christmas celebrating is going to be meaningful, it will be so mostly because of what happens to us on the inside as we celebrate the season. A new reading of the text suggests a whole new internal motivation and spiritual resource for celebrating Christmas differently.

It challenges us to open our own living rooms for Jesus, making room for him not in the barn, not in the inn, but in our living rooms, right where the family lives, where the pets roam, where we work and sleep and play and eat – even when our homes are packed full of guests. If a home in Bethlehem could make room for Jesus in the hustle and bustle of census time, surely we can do it in the hustle and bustle of the Christmas season.

This year I don't want to imagine Jesus lying out in a barn while we prepare our Christmas celebrations and go through the activities of the season. And I don't want to limit the worship part of Christmas to a few reverent trips out to that stable – you know, once or twice during church services and maybe Christmas Eve or Christmas morning before we open gifts.

Rather, I want to imagine Jesus living in our house as we celebrate. I want to imagine him going shopping with me and helping me be kind to the people in the crowded stores. I want to imagine him helping me choose appropriate gifts to express love to those around me. I want to imagine him joining me in the kitchen as I prepare part of our family meal. I want to imagine him *present* – not out there in the barn. After all, they called him Emmanuel, God *with us* – with us not only on Christmas Eve and Christmas morning, but through all the hustle and bustle of the season.

The "Good" Samaritan

Luke 10:25-37

Once upon a time I was told that parables are "earthly stories with heavenly meanings." Much later I realized that they are often "heavenly stories with earthly meanings." Once upon a time, interpreters believed that parables were "allegories about Christian theology." Much later they decided that "every parable makes one and only one point."

If we read them only as artifacts from the first century, meaningless unless interpreted in the light of their original context, they lose their power to inform and encourage, confront and convict, puzzle and clarify. Yet if we abandon the first century context of meaning and turn them loose to speak freely and differently to each interpreter, they can too easily become playthings with which we do whatever we like (and we never like it when they challenge our own convictions and our own lives).

Somehow parables, and in particular the parables of Jesus preserved in the Gospels, resist all our attempts to squeeze them into a common mould. And so it behooves us as interpreters to be:

- as informed as possible about first century language and culture, yet equally attuned to the secrets in our own hearts;
- as careful as possible to use tried and true methods of biblical interpretation, yet equally ready to be creative and open to surprises;
- as attuned as we can be to the voice of Jesus and the biblical authors, yet just as ready to hear the voice of the Spirit (or of our brother and sister) saying, "I think this parable is talking to you!"

And sometimes these can only be kept in balance if we first deconstruct our own assumptions and free the parables to "start over" in our interpretations. Let's test how that might happen with the so-called "Parable of the Good Samaritan."

Now even that title needs to be examined. Does it do justice to the parable? Or does it set us off on the wrong foot altogether, almost ensuring that we will miss the main point? If we're thinking about the *content* of the parable, I suppose the normal English title will do, for we all know the story and would all agree that the Samaritan turned out to be a good man (though our titles would more closely mirror Jesus', his interlocutor's and Luke's perspectives if we labeled the man a "Merciful Samaritan" or a "Loving Samaritan" or a "Neighborly Samaritan"). Yet if we are thinking about Jesus' *strategy* in telling the parable, then the usual title sets us off on the wrong track altogether. It creates in us the expectation that yet another Samaritan will live up to his good reputation. I've heard of *Good Samaritan* service organizations, *Good Samaritan* clubs, *Good Samaritan* schools, *Good Samaritan* hospitals ... why not? Everyone knows that Samaritans are the most wonderful, loving, caring people on earth! Who wouldn't want Samaritans as neighbors? Who wouldn't want to be just like them?

But Jesus' strategy was not to pick a perfect example of merciful loving-kindness and let him demonstrate the right way to treat people in need. Jesus' strategy was to shock his hearers by taking the least likely candidate for kindness (at least according to *their* distorted expectations) and portray him as the unexpected care-giver. Jesus' strategy was to shock his hearers.

The problem with hearing the parable of the "Good Samaritan" today is that the parable doesn't shock us anymore. Of course Samaritans are good, compassionate, always ready to help strangers in need. Everyone knows that.

Ironically, the parable of the so-called "Good Samaritan" has sort of self-destructed. It has created a positive image of Samaritans, and so eliminated the shock value that made the parable work in the first place. Put another way, the parable of the Good Samaritan works only if we reject the assumptions that the parable itself has led us to make.

Perhaps a new sort of shock treatment is necessary to allow the parable to speak its message again. What if we re-told the parable this way:

The Parable of the Bad Samaritan

A man was going down from Jerusalem to Jericho, when he fell into the hands of robbers. They stripped him of his clothes, beat him and went way, leaving him half-dead. A priest happened to be going down the same road, and when he saw the man, he passed by on the other side. So, too, a Levite, when he came to the place and saw him, passed by on the other side.

But a Samaritan, as he traveled that way, saw him and cautiously approached the bleeding body. Then he noticed something that neither of the other travelers had observed. The injured man's robe was lying not far from the body, apparently dropped by the robbers in their haste to get away. The Samaritan looked both ways to make sure he was not being watched and then hastily picked up the garment. It was an expensive robe, slightly dirty, but otherwise in good condition. Fearing that the injured man might recover and later report him, he checked once more to make certain that no one was watching and then gave the body a hefty shove down the slope and over the cliff. He did not stay to watch but heard the body crash on the rocks below.

The Samaritan stuffed the robe into his bag and then hurried on to Jericho. There he sold the robe for sixteen denarii. He smiled as he thought to himself. The valuable garment had once belonged to an ordinary Jew. Then it had passed into the hands of Jewish robbers. How easily it could have ended up in the hands of Jewish religious leaders! But by a stroke of fortune, it had come to him, a Samaritan.

He chuckled under his breath, "Tough luck, Jews! Serves you right!" And he went on his way laughing.

Now, that is of course not exactly what Jesus said. Yet there is *something* more faithful about this re-telling than just another re-reading of the familiar cadences of the old story. This one at least shocks! So did the original. How often has our reading of the text done that?

So how do we hear what Jesus really said, and yet hear it in a way that takes into account what the original hearers would *really* have heard, as Jesus told this tale of racism and neighborliness? Clearly we need to revise some of our assumptions about Samaritans, or at least about Jewish prejudices about them. As surely as we link the adjectives "good" or "merciful" with the ethnic designation "Samaritan," the Jews, and particularly the scrupulous pharisaical scribes, would have supplied adjectives like "hateful," "unclean," "religiously perverted," and "racist." If Jesus had chosen a Roman torturer as his model of compassionate care, his parable would have been no more shocking! Can you imagine how the scrupulous scribe must have choked when Jesus made a hated Samaritan instead of a holy Pharisee into the hero of the day?!

So who were these pharisaical scribes who had such evaluations of the Samaritans? Some of our stereotypes of them are accurate to the way they are portrayed in the New Testament. They were scrupulous about religious cleanliness. They were over-scrupulous about legal correctness. And they were ethnocentric (if not racist). The combination of all these is what made this scribe the perfect foil for Jesus as he taught one of his most important lessons – what it means to love one's neighbor.

What is just as important to remember, if we want to hear this parable as Jesus intended it, is that the Samaritans were typically and sometimes quite accurately characterized as having the same faults as the pharisaical Jews. It is hard to say who hated whom more: the Jews the Samaritans, or the Samaritans the Jews.

With that as background information, perhaps we can recapture the effect of Jesus' parable if we try to hear the parable as the Pharisee would have heard it, if we try to re-capture what was going on in his mind as Jesus was speaking to him.

Remember, he thought Jesus' story was going to help him figure out who his neighbor is, who it was that he was required by law to love.

Jesus begins: "A man was going down from Jerusalem to Jericho, when he fell into the hands of robbers. They stripped him of his clothes, beat him and went way leaving him half dead."

So what is going on in the Pharisees' minds? Perhaps something like this:

> Good set up! I love these legal puzzles. I bet this man's neighbor is going to come down the road. I wonder if his neighbor loves him or hates him. One thing is certain, there

won't be any "neighbors" living along this robber-infested road.

They should do something about those robbers – dirty, rotten scoundrels, mostly foreigners, you can be sure of that.

Why can't those hateful Roman troops raid their strongholds and clean up that road? Maybe a few Roman troops would die in the raid, too. What a pity that would be!

Now, why did Jesus say "half-dead"? O well, let's see what happens next.

"A priest happened to be going down the same road, and when he saw the man, he passed by on the other side."

That figures! What else would you expect from a priest? They are so busy with their sacrifices and ceremonies, they can hardly be expected to get their hands dirty helping an ordinary Jew. Stuck-up clergy!

O, now I see about the "half-dead." He probably thought he could justify himself with his ceremonial laws. He probably imagined that the risk of touching a possibly dead body was too great a risk to take. It would hinder his ministry. And of course the ceremonies are everything!

But Jesus is continuing …

"So too, a Levite, when he came to the place and saw him, passed by on the other side."

That figures! Those Levites are so busy reading their Levitical laws. I wonder how they always manage to jump over the text that says they should love their neighbor. They live off everyone else's generosity, but somehow have no generosity themselves to give back. They follow the priests in everything, even in ignoring the law!

Well, there's the two bad examples. Can't imagine who the third person will be. Presumably someone who does, in fact, stop and help. I know I would have stopped, assuming of course that the injured man was a Jew. I know the law!

So who will the third person be? Who will Jesus choose as his good example? After a Priest and a Levite it will probably be a lay Jew. It might even be a lawyer. I sure hope the crowds are paying attention.

"But a Samaritan, as he traveled came to where the man was; and when he saw him, he took pity on him ..."

A Samaritan ... one of those dirty scoundrels?

You've gone too far this time, Teacher! If you think we are going to take that from you, you have another guess coming.

On the other hand, what if the injured man is a Samaritan? Now there's an interesting thought. After all, this is supposed to be a story about loving your neighbor. The injured man is probably the neighbor of this traveling Samaritan.

Maybe those robbers should come back while he's bending over the injured man, and push them both over the cliff.

What's that Jesus is saying?

"He bandaged the wounds."
"He took him to an inn." (To which the Pharisee says, "You
      mean a *Jewish* inn?")
"He paid for the expenses."

Now that's going way to far! I don't go much for this mixing of races myself. Why don't those Samaritans stay in their own country? If it isn't the foreigners who do the robbing, it's the foreigners who get robbed. Well, at least this dangerous road is good for something.

Maybe word will get around, and we can get this place cleaned up once.

What's that Jesus is asking?

"Who acted like a neighbor?"

Well, the one who had mercy of course! (He didn't think he could get me to say the S-word, did he?)

But what does this have to do with me?

I would have stopped, that is if I could be sure the man was a Jew. I thought Jesus was going to help me define my neighbor. What a dumb answer.

Well, at least I'm okay. I love my neighbors . . .

- not the robbers, of course.
- and of course not the Romans ...
- well I must say not the priests either,
- nor the Levites for that matter.
- I most certainly do not love the Samaritans,
- and I've got a lot of trouble with this teacher who believes in race-mixing!

But my neighbor? Of course I love my neighbor.
I wonder why Jesus didn't stick to the question?

Well, perhaps the parable still has the power to shock a little. And all the more if we try to imagine whom Jesus might have lifted out as his hero of compassion today.

Would it be a violent drug-dealer? Perhaps a mass murderer? Maybe an international terrorist? Come to think of it, maybe it would be a pharisaical scribe! After all, it would surely be someone whom we would least expect. Which means, of course, that Jesus wouldn't pick one of us: he couldn't, because then the parable wouldn't work. It wouldn't shock anyone. Everyone knows that we are well known for our caring, merciful readiness to help both neighbor and enemy! Right?

Two Sons and a Running Father

Luke 15:11-32

One day Jesus was enjoying a party! He did that often, especially when there were lots of sinners around. In Jesus' day, these people were a lot more fun to be with than religious people. The religious people also invited Jesus to their feasts, but it seems they always did it with hidden agendas. Perhaps they wanted to be able to drop names, to impress others by having the famous teacher grace their dining room table. Or, more likely, they wanted to find subtle ways of tearing at Jesus' reputation, of finding a way to discredit him or even bring formal charges against him.

It seems that wherever Jesus went, the religious people were always there, spying on him, making sure he behaved, and trying to figure out why he associated with all the wrong people – tax collectors and sinners, as they were usually called by the watchdogs of purity and piety.

This day the religious watchdogs grumbled openly, saying in Jesus' presence, "This man welcomes sinners and eats with them!" But Jesus did not let the religious elite wreck the party. He just kept right on celebrating and at the same time called on the spoilsports to reconsider their attitudes. How nice it would be if they could truly join the party!

Story time

And precisely how did Jesus call on them to rethink their attitudes? He did it, as he did so often, by telling stories, parables that challenged and provoked the hearers. This time, Jesus used three parables to call his hearers to refashion their world views, to invite them to loosen up and enjoy the favor of their loving Heavenly Father. The only problem was, the religious elite didn't even know their Heavenly Father was loving.

They thought of God more as a stingy and demanding boss – at least that's how Jesus characterized them in the third story he told that day.

The first story Jesus told was of a shepherd who loved his flock, his whole flock, so much that even though he had nintety-nine well-behaved sheep who stayed in the pen where they belonged, he wasn't satisfied until he had found the one sheep that had gone astray. And when he found it, he threw a great party! It cost him far more than the one sheep he could have left out there in the cold. Who cares? He loved his sheep so much, he was willing to kill the fatted calf to celebrate the herd that was complete again.

I think the religious people loved that story, at least the part about them being so well-behaved and safe and secure in the fold. But then the perceptive ones might have been bothered by the story a bit, too. The shepherd of course stood for God. The lost sheep was of course someone who did not follow the law. Well, that would mean the party at the end was grossly overdone! And they sure hoped Jesus was not trying to justify his present carousing with all those sinners.

Before they could put it all together, Jesus had another story for them. This time it was a woman with ten coins. Trouble is, one had disappeared somehow. And she wouldn't stop hunting until she had scoured the whole place. But she found it! She promptly blew the whole piggy bank to throw a party with her friends. That's how happy she was to find the one lost coin. Perhaps the Pharisees were scratching their heads a bit harder by now. A woman couldn't possibly stand for God. And how can anyone love a coin that much? And surely Jesus wouldn't be in favor of loving money at all, would he? And what a waste! Rather leave the coin lost than spend all ten for a party. And why is Jesus always talking about parties anyway?

But they had little time to figure that one out before Jesus started on story number three. It's a much more detailed story, and one not only about the lost being found. It is also about what happened after the party was underway. And it shows that God was not satisfied with the return of a lost son. God also wanted to win back the son who never left home.

What's in a name?
Tradition has dubbed this story, "The Prodigal Son." I think it got its name from the Pharisees, or maybe from church people who share some of their faults. For it is hard to think of a less appropriate name:

- As though Jesus was telling a story so that everyone would recognize how bad one of the boys in this family was;
- Or as though Jesus only cared about the faults of the younger son (who confessed them), and not of the older son (who didn't);
- Or as though Jesus didn't really mean to highlight the loving father at all, when in fact he is the only character who is there at the beginning, at the middle, and at the end, always expressing his tremendous love for both of his boys, even though both of them abuse it, and only one confesses his fault.

I think most of us know the general lines of the story. It's about two sons, the younger one chomping at the bit for some lively adventures, the older one slaving away at home and complaining about his hard work, his boring existence, his wasteful brother, and his far-too-generous father. The younger son is driven to repentance when his money runs out and he is left friendless and hungry, working for a pig farmer. The older son never does repent; he just complains. But the father never stopped looking out for the returning adventurer, and never stops reaching out to the hard-working, critical older son. And the story ends without ending. The father is still appealing to his older son to come join the party. But we don't know what he'll decide.

And that's how Jesus leaves it with the Pharisees as well. They felt good at first. Surely they were among the ninety-nine sheep that never went astray. Perhaps they felt almost as good to be considered among the nine coins that never got lost. But in the third story there is only one alternative to the sinful so-called prodigal. Surely Jesus isn't comparing them to the older brother!? Surely Jesus doesn't believe their hearts also needed changing?!

We know the story so well, it is hard to hear it in a new way. And it is even more difficult to know how it applies to us, especially if we're sure we're not half as bad as "the prodigal son" was.

I want us to consider a way of reading the story that might not have occurred to us before. Is this story really about a sinful son and all the wrongs he committed? The Pharisees would have loved to believe this story was really about how bad the younger son was, and how badly that son needed to repent. That way they wouldn't have to deal with the curve ball Jesus threw in at the end, the part about the older son, the part that called their own faithfulness into question.

What did the younger son do wrong?

I want to suggest that this parable isn't about right and wrong at all — that is, not if we measure right and wrong by some kind of objective legal standard or moral code. In fact, I was fascinated to encounter some research once indicating that we can't be sure the younger son ever broke a single law!

It wasn't against the law to ask for his share of the estate. The father could always say "No" if he wanted to.

It wasn't against the law to pack up and leave home. Well, as the modern translations make clear, he did more than pack a suitcase. Where he was going he had more use for cash than fields, so he sold everything and stashed the proceeds in his carry-on. But he didn't break any laws doing that.

And it wasn't against the law to move to a distant country. Why not? Lots of young people move to new places. Risky, maybe, but not illegal!

He squandered his wealth in wild living. That's how the story continues. Well, I suppose that's on the borderline. Clearly, it wasn't prudent, but can we be sure he did anything illegal? Of course, he should have done some better financial planning, maybe invested in a good pension plan. But did he really do something that was technically illegal or immoral? Where's there a law that says you always have to be reasonable and plan ahead? Is it against the law to enjoy life a bit?

Oh yes, there is that one line in the story about squandering his living on prostitutes. Ah, but how can we be sure he really did that? The line about prostitutes comes from the older brother. Did he really know what his brother had done with the money? Or was he just making that up? Can we trust the judgmental, self-righteous (and maybe just a little bit jealous) older brother to accurately describe how the prodigal son had lived?

Well, there probably was some truth in it. Even the younger son had to admit he wasn't spotless. But he could easily have found some defenses for his behavior, had be been so inclined. Still, whether he broke laws or not, his life hit the skids eventually.

A severe famine came over the whole country. And exactly at the time he ran out of money, too! Sure, he should have prepared for the possibility, but how could he know that there would be an economic downturn? We can't blame the younger son for the famine, can we?

And then the part about the pigs. Of course that was a disgrace for a Jew, but he wasn't eating the meat. No chance! They wouldn't even give him the slop for the pigs.

If we really look closely, it's pretty hard to prove that the younger son actually broke any laws. So why does he confess from the bottom of his heart, "Father, I have sinned against heaven and against you?"

It's all about relationships

I think the answer is that he understood what really counts in the family of God. What counts above all is relationships! These (according to Jesus) count far more than how technically right or wrong a person lives – more, for that matter, than slaving away for the father "all these years." Carrying out commands is not the bottom line. This is what the older brother apparently never understood. He challenged his father with the claim, "Look! All these years I've been slaving for you and never disobeyed your orders." Maybe he was right, but unfortunately for him, that simply didn't count for much! Relationships are the important thing.

Let's look at the parable again. But instead of asking, "Which laws were technically broken?" what if we ask, "Which relationships were abused?" If that's the question, then the whole parable looks different. Then neither of the sons can come up with much to defend themselves. To ask for one's share of the estate didn't break any law, but it was still an unimaginable thing to do. It was as if the young man were complaining to his father, "You are living too long. I don't want to wait any more! I want to get something out of life now. I don't want to wait until you're dead!"

And the older brother didn't do much when he later complained, "All these years I've been slaving for you!" "Look how long I've been waiting to become the boss! How much longer do you intend to live, Dad?" The issue is not obeying commands. The issue is relationships, and the relationship to their father was disdained by both of the sons.

The relationship between the two sons was no better. The older son accuses his father, "When this son of yours who has squandered your property with prostitutes comes home, you kill the fatted calf for him!"

129

"This son of yours" – as if he wanted to make things clear: "He's not my brother – not any more. If you haven't rejected him by now, I sure have."

Of course, the younger son kind of deserved this rejection. Both sons knew what would happen if the inheritance was divided after the death of the father. The older brother would get two portions and the younger son only one. That was all regulated by the inheritance laws. Both knew as well that when a father decided to divide up the property while he was still alive, it was so that he could divide things fifty-fifty. The younger son had dared to beg for that. And so he ended up with a considerably larger portion of the inheritance than he would otherwise have been able to get. So he hadn't actually broken a law, but he had sure put a strain on family relationships.

And what about the other things he did – selling the land, moving away, wasting the property? That was unheard of in his culture. Impossible. If a father chose to divide up the property while he was still alive, it was taken for granted that the children would support their parents in their old age – so taken for granted that they didn't even need laws to regulate it!

The younger son had acted disgracefully. Actually, both of them had! The difference between them was that the younger son recognized what he had done and came back to repent. This parable is not finally about how terrible things can become for those who fall into sin. It is rather about how important it is to preserve loving relationships and, when necessary, to rebuild the ones that break down.

We've always known that this parable portrays a young man who sinned immeasurably, who reached the bottom, and who was totally dependent on the forgiveness of a loving Father. But exactly how he sinned, what it meant to hit the bottom – here is where the parable challenges us to revise our thinking. In terms of breaking laws, the son was far less guilty than we might suppose. Where he fell short was in relationships. That's surely why his confession acknowledged his sin "against heaven and against you." The issue is not objective guilt, but broken relationships.

Is this parable about us?

If this parable is going to speak to us, we need to move beyond questions of objective guilt. If the parable provokes us only to ask, "What have I done wrong? Which law did I break?" then we will probably be able to escape the force of it. Then it turns out to be about other people – prodigals, down-and-outers, ultra-legalists. But if we ask the far more important questions, "How are things between me and my God? How are things between me and my brothers and sisters?" then this parable can still confront and challenge us and, depending on our response, condemn or console us.

Of course, for most Christians it is more comfortable to divert the whole topic to moral correctness. It's so much easier to maintain blamelessness before the law, or measure how hard we have slaved in the fields as the older brother did. But when we do, we run the risk of siding with the Pharisees in Jesus' audience. And remember, it was the tax collectors and sinners who were enjoying the party with him!

When we focus on the law we're constantly tempted to say, "I never disobeyed your orders." If we focus on relationships we are invited to say, "Father, I have sinned against heaven and against you," and when we do, God throws a party for us!

This parable is about two sons struggling with priorities, struggling to discover what the father never doubts from beginning to end, and that is what the right priorities must be. They must be relationships, relationships in God's family. That's why the father works so hard, and lovingly, and patiently, to restore the relationships that have broken down.

The father

By calling this parable "The Prodigal Son" or sometimes "The Prodigal Sons" we effectively marginalize the father. When we see that everything revolves around relationships, the father is restored to center stage. Some have tried to centralize the father in the parable by re-naming it "The Parable of the Waiting Father." But is it not rather a parable about a running father?

How far was this father willing to go to restore the broken relationships in his family? Here we get some help from Professor Kenneth Bailey. As a professor at the Hebrew University in Jerusalem, one of the things he did was to interpret the parables so that they might speak to his students and to his Muslim teaching colleagues. And as a missionary to Arab peasants, he sought to preach the gospel in the small farming villages around Jerusalem.

The Parable of the Prodigal Son was one that Kenneth Bailey used often to share the good news of Jesus. And since many rural Arabs have a culture that even today is remarkably similar to the culture of the Jews in Jesus' day, Kenneth Bailey sometimes gained insights into the significance of this parable from the Arab farmers with whom he shared the Gospel – insights that he could never have gained in the university library.

Bailey would slowly share the parable and then watch closely how his hearers would respond. To them it was self-evident that this parable was about relationships. These people were not asking, "Was it legal or illegal for the younger son to ask for his share of the inheritance?" Their question was, "How could a son bring such shame on himself and his family? How could he take advantage of family relationships like that?" These people did not ask, "Was it legal or illegal to sell the land and move to another country with the money?" Their question was more like, "How could anyone treat his family so shamefully?"

And so it went through the entire story. But the biggest surprise of all was the reaction that Kenneth Bailey observed as he told the part of the story where the Father ran to meet the returning prodigal. His hearers responded in amazement: "The father, too? Would he also bring shame on himself?"

"How's that?" asked Bailey.

"Because an old man wouldn't run!"

"Why not?" asked Bailey.

"Because he would have to lift up his robe!"

Suddenly Kenneth Bailey found an answer to a question that had troubled him. His Muslim colleagues at the university in Jerusalem had often challenged his claim that God's forgiveness was a costly thing, paid for by God's own grace. They had often replied, "But just look at the Parable of the Prodigal Son. There the father simply pronounced a word of forgiveness. It didn't cost him anything!"

Now Kenneth Bailey understood something new. The prodigal son was on his way back home. What could he expect from the people of the village? They would mock him, laugh at him, and scorn him. The children would throw stones or spit at him; some would turn their backs. This young man who brought so much shame on his family would never again find his place in the village.

But the people of the village saw something totally unexpected. The father who was so scorned by his younger son did something himself that would make him a laughingstock. He picked up his garments and ran! He made a fool of himself. That was unheard of for a man his age in that culture. Now the children would mock him, too.

And so these two, father and son, would come together back into the village, both objects of scorn. The father was willing to sacrifice his own honor so that his son would not have to come home alone in disgrace. Kenneth Bailey gained new insight, not only into this parable, but into the whole New Testament message of grace. Grace is a loving God, taking on our shame and exchanging it for glory!

Yes, it did cost God something: honor. And that, ultimately, is what the Parable of the Prodigal Son is about. It is about a prodigal son recognizing the priority of relationships. But even more it is about a father for whom relationships are so important that he's willing to risk his honor, willing to submit to scorn, willing to break all the rules of propriety if only relationships with prodigals can be rebuilt.

What a generous waste!

Have you ever thought about the word "prodigal?" It means "generously wasteful," and so we apply it to the younger son who lived his frivolous life wasting his money on things that really didn't count, and in the end didn't make him happy either. And sometimes we apply it to the older brother who wasted a perfectly good opportunity to enjoy the love, the security, not to mention the parties, in a wonderful home – wasted it by slaving and complaining. Have you ever thought of calling this "The Parable of the Prodigal Father?" What a generous waste to kill a fatted calf to celebrate one little lamb that is found! What a generous waste to spend ten coins on a party to celebrate finding one that was lost! And what a generous waste to throw a party for a son who has just frittered away half your fortune on . . . well, on nothing really! But God's like that.

Here's a father willing to throw away his honor, if necessary, to welcome a returning son. He'll come begging a self-righteous son to quit working so hard and join the music and dancing. And he'll do it, even if there's not much chance the son will actually come. What a waste! But if even one sheep is found, one coin is found, one child comes home – well, he would spend his whole fortune to make that happen. That's just how God is!

What a perfect parable for Jesus to tell while eating with tax collectors and sinners. What a perfect parable to challenge and confront in all cultures and all centuries, as long as there are people who scorn a relationship with God – as long as there are people still learning that such a relationship is infinitely more important to God than being technically morally correct, or slaving away in our father's vineyards.

A loving relationship with us is more important to God than God's own honor and all the rules of propriety. And God waits patiently until we decide that a loving relationship with our Father is more important to us than defending our honor. More important than being good. More important than slaving away for God. More important than pursuing a kind of happiness that leaves us empty and unfulfilled, while all the treasures of heaven are waiting for us to enjoy.

Sure, this parable speaks to the down-and-outers who have hit the bottom, grasping for anything that might mean the rescue of a ruined life. There's good news here for those who feel like the younger son starving near the pigs' trough.

Sure, this parable speaks to those whose wasteful and frivolous lifestyles haven't caught up with them yet, but who have a deep longing for something better than the kind of happiness they are so desperately chasing. For such people there's good news here.

Sure, this parable speaks to those who stand up proudly, claiming, "I have never disobeyed a single one of your commands," and then complain about those who work less, spend more, or enjoy life more easily. Maybe some of us fit fairly well into this category. If so, there's good news for us here today.

But surely this parable also has a powerful message for all of us who find ourselves somewhere between all those extremes, somewhere between very good and very bad, somewhere between lost and found, somewhere between the pig troughs in a foreign land and living at the center of God's loving family. Wherever we are on any of these scales, there is good news for us here today. Today God is saying to us, "I'm ready to throw another party. Just give me half a reason and we'll kill the fatted calf!"

Whenever we take just one step towards home, we can be sure our loving Father will come running towards us. He'll throw his arms around us, welcome us home, put a ring on our finger, and put shoes on our feet. And there'll be a party in our honor.

A Friend in Need

Luke 11:5-8

Sometimes just one little word makes all the difference in the world! Somewhere, someone reached the (unfortunately incorrect) conclusion that the Greek word *anaideia* meant "persistence." As a result, for the better part of two millennia, Christians have been told by countless preachers (and until recently by almost every Bible translation) that the key to effective prayer is being *persistent* enough. We picture God as an unjust judge who couldn't care less what we want (cf. Luke 18:1-8; cf. the next contribution to this collection), and so we feel constrained to play the role of a persistent widow, badgering an unjust judge into giving in. We picture God as a tired grouch who keeps hollering from his bed, "Leave me alone and let me get some sleep" (cf. Luke 11:5-8; see below), and so we feel constrained to play the role of a man persistently knocking and begging, refusing to take "No" for an answer. Well, if we don't exactly picture God like that, we still think these parables are about what God is like, sort of.

Somehow, we manage to ignore almost everything else the Bible teaches about God and about prayer. We forget that the "persistent pray-ers" were the ones *mocked* by God's prophet, Elijah. "Shout louder! ... Maybe he is sleeping and must be awakened" (1 Kings 18:27). We ignore the model of Jesus (and Paul for that matter) who both prayed earnestly three times, then concluded that God's intention was to say "No" and provide enough grace to accept that answer (Mark 14:41; 2 Cor. 12:8,9). We even forget that Jesus taught his disciples a way of praying that distinguished it from pagan praying precisely because it did not depend on endless repetitions to be effective (Matt. 6:7,8).

135

Everywhere else in the Bible, prayer is all about expressing faith in a generous God, not outlasting a reluctant God; it is about submitting to God's will, not trying to change it. Yet generations of Christians have lived with the guilt of accepting the blame for prayers going unanswered. "If only you had been persistent enough, God might have said, *Yes*" (we are told, or we tell ourselves). But what does all this have to do with one little word? Here's the story:

> A man, desiring to feed an unexpected guest, tries to borrow bread from his friend. He knocks (whoops, the tradition made up that part!), makes his request, and waits … but no one appears at the door with the needed provision. The problem is not that there's no bread in his friend's house. The problem is that it's midnight and his friend has no interest in getting out of bed at such an impossible hour. But the would-be host persists. Does he knock three times, ten times, fifty times? Who knows. Whatever it takes, he manages it. He outlasts his lazy friend, who finally decides he'll get even less sleep if he stays in bed. Getting up he gives the bread … not because of the friendship, but because he can't stand the knocking anymore. Persistence pays!

That's how we read the little story Jesus tells in Luke 11:5-8. And that is just how it is with prayer (we are told), even though a thousand other texts in the Bible come rushing in to contradict our conclusion. Guilt swells up in us for all the times we gave up too soon. We imagine we are being true to Scripture by thinking of prayer as outlasting God. (God would rather stay in bed and be left alone!)

And when prayers are answered, we should feel good about our persistence, shouldn't we? Yet somehow imagining God turning over in bed and saying, "I'm sick and tired of you asking," then staggering to the door and saying, "Here. Take the bread and leave me alone!" Well, that doesn't really fill our hearts with joy. So we take the hard-won bread and feel bad that we asked.

Or maybe we are rescued by our common sense and remind ourselves that God really couldn't possibly be like the sleepy friend. We then reformulate the meaning of this parable into something like: "Effectiveness in prayer depends on the adequacy of our approach to

God, who would love to give but waits to see how serious we are about the request." There, that's almost what the parable says and surely a more acceptable picture of God.

And yet our image of God still haunts us, especially when we pray for something with all the seriousness and persistence we can muster and our request is still not granted. We imagine God saying: "I really wanted to give you your request all along, but you were not quite persistent enough. You can't imagine how close you were to getting your request. Better luck next time."

> Even though he will not get up and give him anything because he is his friend, at least because of his persistence he will get up and give him whatever he needs. (Luke 11:8, NRSV).

One word makes all the difference in the world. If only we could get rid of that troublesome word "*persistence*," we could blame our unanswered prayer on someone or something else. But there's that troublesome word! Persistence pays. If we don't get the pay out, there must have been too little persistence. Good thing the would-be *host* in the story didn't give up or he would have gone home empty-handed.

The fact is, there are some very good biblical reasons for wanting to get rid of that word *persistence*. This isn't all about dealing with guilt and finding less strenuous ways to pray.

It seems a bit odd, doesn't it, that Jesus provides his disciples with the so-called "Lord's Prayer" (according to Matthew's Gospel; cf. 6:7-13) so that they will not *mis*understand how prayer works. It is *not* a matter of endless repetitions! That's how "the Gentiles" think it works, says Jesus. "*{They} think they will be heard because of their many words. Do not be like them, for your Father knows what you need before you ask him. This, then, is how you should pray: {the Lord's Prayer}.*" And Luke *seems* to counter with: "Ah, God knows what you need all right, but what good does that do? God wants to get a good night's sleep, doesn't want to be troubled by our petty wishes. It will take more than a good prayer to provoke an answer. If you expect an answer, hang in there. You will only get it, if at all, *because of your many words!*" Odd, isn't it?

It also seems odd that Luke would follow up the "persistent friend" parable with what seems like a blanket promise: "Everyone who asks, receives" (11:10); whatever happened to the prerequisite, the persistent knocking, the repeated begging? And it seems odd as well that Jesus would end the section by reminding us how readily human fathers, *even evil ones*, give good gifts to their children, and *how much more ready* God is to do so if only we'll ask (11:11-13). Whatever happened to the "persistent begging" prerequisite? We're told that Jesus' parable says: if friendship won't get God to budge, try knocking longer and demanding louder; it just might work!

Everything screams for a reinterpretation of Jesus' parable. But what else could it possibly mean? That troublesome word "persistence" is there, right where we don't want it to be! If only we could figure out how to make it go away! Here's the good news: despite everything we've heard in the past, *anaideia* almost certainly does *not* mean persistence. And the parable almost certainly does *not* teach that the effectiveness of prayer depends on us getting all the techniques right and outlasting a reluctant God.

The first hint that a long tradition was about to be overturned came in an article by Alan Johnson. Noting that the word *anaideia* is not found elsewhere in Biblical literature, Johnson researched how the word was used in other Greek literature up to the fifth century C.E. He found only one case where the sense of the word was "enduring" or "persisting" and found no evidence that the word would have been understood this way in the first century.

What then does *anaideia* mean? A number of scholars have reached the conclusion which Johnson himself reached – the word means "shamelessness." It is the would-be host's *shamelessness*, not his *persistence*, that makes the sleeper get up. Other interpreters (including myself) prefer a different view (see below).

What seems clear is that the word *anaidea* is derived from another word *aidos* (meaning shame or sense of shame) and the prefix *an* (a prefix of negation in Greek). If Luke 11 retains the meaning that this combination suggests, then the parable says the sleeper is motivated to get up and give his friend bread by the "non-shame-factor." But what's a "non-shame-factor"?

Several recent English translations (or revisions) are abandoning the older view that the knocker's request is granted because of his *persistence*. Alternatives like *shamelessness* or *boldness* are appearing, either in the text or in footnotes. In my opinion that is only a slight improvement on the traditional view. It still leaves us with some major problems.

Theologically we still have the problem of imagining that prayer works because someone managed to override God's real intentions with manipulative techniques. This view also misunderstands the cultural context of the original parable. It assumes that only a shameless or exceptionally courageous host would dare to ask a friend at midnight for three loaves of bread. *Today* that might be true – a considerate or cowardly friend would far more likely go to the 24-hour grocery store down the street than wake up a sleeping friend! In those days things were different.

The key to unlocking this parable is to determine what role "shame" or "shamelessness" would have played in the actions (or proposed actions) of the various characters.

The parable opens with a challenge to the hearers to try to imagine the unimaginable. English translations usually say, "Suppose ... " It would be closer to Jesus' intentions if we paraphrased it like this. "It is unthinkable, isn't it, that a scenario would unfold like this ... [and then the story is told]." Jesus is not asking his audience to suppose this really happened. He's acknowledging that they can't imagine a story unfolding like this. And it really is an impossible story ... but not for the reasons we might suppose.

A traveler arrives at midnight – unthinkable! Not in those days. Traveling in the evening (or even at night) was not at all unusual, especially in the heat of summer.

He arrives at midnight and expects to be fed – unthinkable! Not in those days. There were no late night fast food chains along the route. And even if the traveler had not been particularly hungry, sharing bread was part of an appropriate welcome, at any time of day or night.

The host has no bread to offer his guest – unthinkable! Not in those days. People usually baked just enough bread for the day. Without preservatives (and of course without freezers) it made little sense to keep a breadbox full, just in case.

He tried to borrow bread from his neighbor at midnight – unthinkable! Not in those days. The obligation to be a good host rested not only with one family, but with the entire village. A guest of the village must not go to bed hungry – not if there was bread somewhere in the village. (Remember there were no 24-hour grocery stores!)

The entire story seems improbable *to us*, that is, everything except the behavior of the sleepy man. We have no trouble imagining him say,

"Do not bother me; the door has already been locked and my children are with me in bed." "Just what I would be thinking!" we respond. But precisely here, *the first hearers* would have said, "*Unthinkable!*"

In fact our modern translations here are quite misleading. NRSV introduces the sleeper's (proposed) response with the words, "And he answers from within . . ." But the whole point of the parable is that he does not answer like this from within. We are supposed to try (in vain) to *imagine* him answering like this, which of course we cannot do . . . it's unthinkable!

Let me paraphrase the parable to make this clearer:

> It is unthinkable, isn't it, that a scenario would unfold like this: You are in bed; it's midnight. Suddenly you hear your friend at the door asking for bread. A traveler has arrived at his house and he has nothing to offer him. You do indeed have a couple of extra loaves.

So far the hearers are saying, "Okay so far, everything seems normal."

> Now try to imagine yourself telling your friend, "Do not bother me; the door has already been locked and my children are with me in bed."

At that point the hearers would either laugh or gasp. "Can't imagine it!" is their unanimous conclusion. "Nobody would answer like that!" *Why not?* (we ask). "Well there's the shame factor!" *What shame factor?* "Where do you come from?" (our imaginary first century hearers are thinking). "If you replied like that your friend would go to the neighbors and borrow bread from them. And while he was at it, he would say: 'Can you imagine what the guy next door told me! He said he had the bread but was too lazy to get up!' By next morning your reputation would be ruined!"

The final verse of Jesus' parable should be read like this: "Even if the sleepy friend would not get up to help out a friend in need, at least the 'non-shame-factor' would be enough to provoke him to get up and give him everything he needs."

What's a "non-shame-factor?" In this parable it is that which motivates the sleeper to get up and share his bread. He acts for the sake of the honor of his name; he acts so that his honor is preserved, so that he doesn't have to live with the shame of a ruined reputation.

So what is it about the host's behavior that makes all the difference in this parable? Is it his *persistence*? His *boldness*? His *shamelessness*? It's none of the above. This parable is not about what the host has to do to be heard. It's all about the *sleeper*! It's the *anaideia* (the non-shame-factor) of the sleeper, not of the host, that makes the difference. No doubt their friendship would motivate him to get up, but even if not, he would most certainly get up anyway; his own honor is at stake!

Read this way, Jesus' parable fits the larger context of Luke 11 (and the rest of the Bible) perfectly. Just as in Matthew, Luke's version of the Lord's prayer is provided to demonstrate that effective prayer does *not* depend on our techniques or our persistence. We bring our requests to God to demonstrate our trust in and dependence on one who loves us, who knows our needs, and who generously meets them. Even if we could not count on our *loving Father* to meet our needs (which if course we can, since even "evil fathers" do no less; cf. Luke 11:13), there is always the "non-shame-factor" ... God acts for the sake of the honor of God's own name.

God acts, not because petitioners have earned the right to be heard, or have outlasted a reluctant parent, but for the sake of God's honor. What would "the nations" think if God didn't even take care of God's own people?

"Hallowed (honored) be your name" is how the Lord's prayer begins. Our request for daily bread (or for that matter for forgiveness and protection, cf. Luke 11:3-4) does not need to be repeated a million times to overcome the reluctance of a God who hates to be disturbed. Our prayers are heard because we are invited to call God "Our Father" and because God's concern and ours are the same, God's name is to be honored.

The Widow and the Judge

Luke 18:1-8

God hears our prayers!

We confess along with the Scriptures and the saints throughout the ages, "God hears our prayers!" And then when we are alone (and honest) we quietly add, "Well, sometimes – at least for other people. But why doesn't God hear my prayers?" "Call to me and I will answer you," we read in Jeremiah 33:3. And if we are honest, we silently add, "But I've been praying so long. God sure hasn't answered my prayer!"

And alongside the wonderful promises that God listens to our prayers, we remember those other passages that seem to say, "But of course one needs to pray with persistence. God isn't simply at our beck and call, you know!" Among these are Luke's parables about prayer: the one about the friend asking for bread at midnight (see previous chapter), and the one about the widow and the judge. Those who have read the previous chapter know that I don't support the traditional interpretation of Luke 11:5-8. Now we want to take a look at Luke 18:1-8. Jesus tells how a mistreated widow, through persistent badgering and maybe even the threat of a physical attack, coerces an evil judge to give her justice – an example for us on how to get God to answer our prayers. Or have we misunderstood this parable as well?

"Grant me justice!"

It's quite a gripping story, and not completely unrealistic in the world of the first century. In larger towns there might have been a tribunal of judges, so that normal citizens were somewhat protected from the caprice of not-so-just justices. But in smaller villages a single judge would settle legal disputes. And if that single magistrate was not entirely committed to fair judgments, it really could happen that a helpless widow had little chance against an influential and probably rich opponent (i.e. one far more capable of "influencing" a judge with personal favors). At any rate, the story Jesus tells is about just such a situation with just such a judge.

The judge is described first in the story. He cares little about God, about justice, about people in need, perhaps even about his own reputation. And that's not just the opinion of the narrator. He describes himself that way: "I don't fear God or care about people." Then we hear about the widow. She has come with a presumably legitimate complaint: "Grant me justice." As a widow, she has no husband to plead her cause. Apparently she has neither father nor son either, for she stands there alone. In her culture that means her chances are small, especially with a judge who cares neither for the helpless, nor for justice itself.

And yet somehow in the end the judge reverses even his own declared intentions, saying, "I will see that she gets justice." What ever brings about the change of heart? Does her bitter plea finally touch his heart strings? No. Are her arguments so persuasive? No. Does her opponent concede that the widow was in the right? No. The fact is, nothing changes his heart. He starts out selfish and he ends up selfish. What happens is that he discovers his own best interests will in the end be better served if he reverses his course of action.

She must be a feisty woman. She just won't accept "No" for an answer. The narrator says, "She kept coming!" The judge says, "This widow keeps bothering me." Finally, he can't stand it anymore. He decides he's better off granting her request, so that [translated literally] "she won't 'blacken my eye' with her coming." What is he afraid of?

There are three possibilities:

1. Perhaps the mere sight of this woman makes him cover his face with his hands and cry, "Oh, no! Not this widow again! Get out of my sight! I can't stand the sight of you!" In other words, he "blackens his own eye" at the sight of the persistent widow.
2. Perhaps he fears she will literally attack him! That's how it's translated by Eugene Peterson: "I'm going to be beaten black-and-blue by her pounding." In other words, the "black eye" would be the woman's handiwork.

3. Perhaps he recognizes that his reputation is at stake. He doesn't care one wit about people's *need*, but might care what people *think of* him. Perhaps he notices which way the wind is blowing. If the support of the village shifts to the helpless widow, he'd better do something to keep from getting a black eye (a ruined reputation).

And so in the end he helps her. He hadn't wanted to, but he finds himself no match for her persistence, her threat of abuse, or the hard-earned sympathy she has won over (or maybe she has mastered all three forms of coercion!). I can imagine him bellowing (or perhaps muttering), "All right, all right. I'm judging in your favor; now get out of here and don't bother me again!"

And that is just what prayer is like!

There we have it: God hears our prayers. All we have to do is pester, badger and threaten until God can't stand it anymore, just as we see illustrated in this story. Well, not exactly the way it works in this story. Well, to be more accurate, nothing at all like we read in the story. Fortunately, our common sense rescues us and we put a huge question mark over this whole way of interpreting the parable. But then someone reminds us of the verse that precedes the parable, and our worst fears are confirmed. We are indeed supposed to interpret the parable as a description of how prayer works. "Jesus told his disciples a parable to show them that they should always pray and not give up." There it is in black and white.

And so we conclude that we really are supposed to learn about prayer as we observe the widow's way of dealing with the judge. Throwing common sense to the wind, we start our persistent begging, despite all the clear warnings in Scripture that this is not at all what prayer is supposed to be like (e.g. 1 Kings 18:27; Matt. 6:7,8). And when prayer doesn't work even then, the temptation is great to conclude that prayer simply doesn't work, period. Disheartened, we quit. Or if we're as persistent as the widow – disheartened, we keep on badgering God.

Doesn't the parable just cry out for a reinterpretation? How can God, who is nothing at all like the judge in the story, require us to act just like the widow to get our requests heard? But if we are not supposed to treat God as the widow does the judge, how does this parable teach us about prayer?

From lesser to greater

Interpreters often speak of comparisons, metaphors or parables as arguing "from lesser to greater." This proposal recognizes that the judge is nothing at all like God. Truth is, one can hardly imagine anyone more *unlike* God than this parable's judge. Twice we are informed that he cares neither about divine justice nor about human need. And everyone listening to Jesus' parable knew that Israel's God was just the opposite. They understood him to be the very standard of justice, with an immeasurable kindness that is poured out most generously on the helpless. That's God's reputation and it's something God is concerned to preserve (Ps. 106:8; Isa. 48:11; Ezek. 20:9,14,44).

We are not supposed to compare God with this judge, and most certainly not equate them. But we can still argue "from lesser to greater." If even the godless misanthropic judge in this story can be moved to give justice, *how much more* will a just and loving God do so? If the desperate measures of a poor helpless widow can make a difference, *how much more* will our prayers move the heart and the hand of God?

Persistent prayer

Now, that helps considerably. Yet it still leaves us wondering what sort of prayers get through to God. If God is totally unlike the judge and if our situation before God is not much like the widow's before the judge, why did Jesus use the parable to teach a lesson about prayer? And what exactly is the point of comparison? The traditional answer goes something like this: we are being called to be persistent. Of course we don't threaten and badger God. We just have to be as persistent as this widow. The widow needed persistence to get through to the judge; we need it to get through to God. Why else would Jesus have told the parable? And besides, the opening verse clearly tells us that this is the point of the parable, to teach us "to always pray and not give up." And then there's Jesus' promise that God responds to those who "cry out to him day and night." Case closed.

But these arguments do not persuade me. God is unlike the judge; we are unlike the widow. Why then should we imitate the widow, crank up the persistence, and thus treat God as though God is like the judge after all? Let's re-imagine Jesus' story. What if God had been the one to whom the widow came for justice? What if, instead of a selfish unjust judge, she had approached the unselfish, loving and kind God of the universe, the one full of justice and gracious to the helpless? What would the widow have had to do to get justice from this judge? Absolutely nothing, except lay her case before him! Why then should we need to do more than that when God *really is* in the place of the judge, and we are in the place of the widow?

Something just does not fit. And the translators, as hard as they try to make it fit, really don't quite succeed. For we are told that, though God's children do cry out to him day and night (persistently?), God doesn't need that. God does *not* keep putting them off (v.7). God grants justice *quickly* (v.8). Why then the need for persistence? Time for a new look at an old story.

Don't give up!

I think we go wrong already in the first verse. We are supposed to learn to "always pray." But we far too quickly imagine that this means repeating our requests over and over, persisting until we've persuaded God to answer. And when we hear "and not give up," we think our reading is confirmed. Pray ten times, and if that doesn't bring results, go on to twenty, and thirty, and fifty, and a hundred. Don't give up! What if you stopped and God was just about to answer the prayer?

The text speaks of "not giving up" but it does not speak of "not giving up *praying*." The expression is not telling us *how long* to pray, but what we would be doing if we didn't pray. Life is hard. Discouragement and despair are never far away, especially when we have powerful opponents and they treat us unfairly. There are times when we really feel like *giving up* – giving up hope, giving up responding to enemies as Jesus taught. But Jesus says, "Don't give up! There's an alternative. Instead of giving up, *pray*!" Which will we choose? If we follow Jesus' counsel, we'll choose prayer every time ("always pray"); and if that is our choice, we will "not give up" (i.e. not despair). Luke 18:1 speaks of prayer as a regular habit; it does not speak about the length of our prayers or the number of repetitions.

In case that didn't come through clearly, let me try it again. We wrongly imagine Jesus putting *this* choice before us: 1) the type of praying that is "not-giving-up" – i.e. the persistent kind; or 2) the type of praying that is "giving-up" – i.e. the one that stops too soon, perhaps because we doubt God will answer, perhaps because we are casual, flippant or lazy.

But Jesus is setting a different choice before us. It's not about "giving-up-praying" vs. "not-giving-up-praying." It is between "praying" and "giving up." Jesus says, "When you are tempted to give up, pray instead! When you are helpless and discouraged, confidently approach the one who responds to the helpless and the discouraged. Come in prayer to the one who responds *quickly*!"

Day and night

But now we must examine another reason people imagine that we're called to persistence in prayer. We've examined two reasons already. The first was the assumption that we're required to mimic the widow; I simply don't believe that is the point of the parable. The second was our (mis)reading of verse 1; I've suggested an alternative. Now comes the third reason: Verse seven speaks of those who call out to God "day and night." The English expression gives the impression we are being counseled to pray *for a long time*; the Greek expression behind it does not!

The two words "day" and "night" could have been written in Greek in three different cases. Had the accusative been used, it would have indicated the length of time – God hears those who pray all day and all night. Had the dative been used, it would have indicated the precise timing of the prayer – God hears prayers at 2:30 AM no less than at 4:45 PM. But Luke uses neither the accusative nor the dative. He uses the genitive. A genitive puts emphasis on the *kind* of prayer that is prayed. God hears a "daytime prayer" and God hears a "nighttime prayer." God is there for us not only at every moment, but for every sort of need.

Jesus' parable speaks of a conflict that requires judicial intervention. It invites us to contemplate the plight of the helpless widow, and then to discern where our situation might be comparable. Perhaps someone is taking advantage of us; we feel helpless, but are assured that we can turn to God. What would a "daytime prayer" be like? I imagine myself accidentally meeting my opponent in a grocery store. I am tempted to mutter, "I'll get you; just you wait and see!" To be honest, I'm tempted to smash his face! What then is a "daytime prayer?" Perhaps: "Lord, teach me your patience! Help me to await your justice, not seek worldly revenge. Transform my priorities, so that bearing faithful witness matters more to me than fighting for my rights." God hears such daytime prayers.

And what would a "nighttime prayer" be like? I imagine myself unable to sleep. The unfair treatment my opponent dishes out weighs heavily on me. Will I spend another sleepless night in self-pity, perhaps planning revenge? Or will I utter my nighttime prayer: "How long, Lord?" And as I cry out, I am reminded of the "souls under the altar" in Revelation 6:9-11. They too cried out "How long?" as they awaited their own vindication. They had faced persecution far more severe than I usually face. And God reassures them (just as Jesus reassures us through Luke's parable): "It won't be long now. Wait just a little longer. I'll intervene quickly; I'll make all things right again soon."

Neither by day nor by night do we need to outlast a reluctant God with our persistent prayers. God has promised justice, and that quickly!

But still we object: "I've prayed for a new car a thousand times and God still hasn't given me one." And God says, "This parable is not about new cars; and besides, the parable doesn't ask you to try to outlast me!" And we respond: "Okay then, I've prayed for far more legitimate and necessary things, even things your Word promises me, but I'm still waiting!" And God says, "This parable isn't about *things* at all; it is about God's justice when we are treated unfairly. And remember, it is not about persistence either." So we say: "Okay then, I was treated unfairly. When are you going to pay my enemy back for what he did? I've brought this request before you hundreds of times." And God responds, "I'll give you justice, but that doesn't mean I'll pay him back. How about if I give you more patience? Help you to love your enemy? Remind you that earthly justice is not the kind I offer? And remember, this is not about persistence!" And so we say: "But even for those things, I've been waiting a long time!" And God says, "I'll respond quickly. Just wait a little longer." And so this text joins so many others in Scripture that remind us that God's timing is different from ours, that in comparison with eternity, our time of waiting is not really that long.

Jesus' final question in our text is this: "When the Son of Man comes, will he find faith on the earth?" The Son of Man is not looking for persistent widows trying to coerce a judge to act. He is looking for those who, by day or night, lay their cause before the Lord with the cry, "How long?" and who believe God's answer: "Soon."

Rehabilitating Thomas

John 20:19-20, 24-31

We call ourselves believers. We call ourselves people of faith. What do we mean by these words? Does it mean that we always believe whole-heartedly, that we have no doubts, that our faith is always strong even when the going is tough?

Our lives often take on a rhythm of believing and then doubting again ... or wanting to believe and finding it very difficult ... or believing when there is good evidence, and then finding our faith slipping away when we no longer see the reasons we believed in the first place.

John's Gospel addresses this phenomenon. His report of the resurrection appearances of Jesus centers on this very theme – on the issue of strong faith and weak faith, on signs and the absence of signs, on conviction and doubt. By it we're helped to answer some difficult questions. What makes faith possible? What's wrong with us when we are plagued with doubt? Are there ways we can help each other believe?

Let's observe how the resurrected Jesus dealt with ten disciples who were together on the evening of the resurrection, and then with Thomas who missed that meeting and had trouble believing.

It has been quite a day! In fact, the day that is now ending will turn out to be the day around which all of history pivots. Today Jesus rose from the dead. But now it is evening, and ten men are together, scared, hiding, keeping the doors locked ... and then Jesus comes. The text is familiar, but it is worth examining again, to make sure we catch what it really says.

On the evening of that first day of the week, when the
disciples were together, with the doors locked for fear of the

Jews, Jesus came and stood among them and said, "Peace be with you!" After he said this, he showed them his hands and side. The disciples were overjoyed when they saw the Lord.

Thomas, one of the twelve, was not with the disciples when Jesus came. When the other disciples told him that they had seen the Lord, he declared, "Unless I see the nail marks in his hands and put my finger where the nails were, and put my hand into his side, I will not believe it."

A week later his disciples were in the house again, and Thomas was with them. Though the doors were locked, Jesus came and stood among them and said, "Peace be with you!" Then he said to Thomas, "Put your finger here; see my hands. Reach out your hand and put it into my side. Stop doubting and believe."

Thomas said to him, "My Lord and my God."

Jesus told him, "Because you have seen me, you have believed; blessed are those who have not seen and yet have believed."

"Jesus did many other miraculous signs in the presence of his disciples, which are not recorded in this book. But these are written that you may believe that Jesus is the Christ, the Son of God, and that by believing you may have life in his name." (John 20:19-20, 24-31)

That's the text. It is a text about believing – about believing or *not* believing. Or maybe we should say about believing *with* or *without* having seen.

It raises questions about the relationship between signs and faith. Are we expected to believe without signs or because of them? Is our faith more genuine if we believe even though we have not seen, or is it okay to see first and then believe? Why do some seem to find it harder to believe than others? Why do we find it harder to believe at some times than at other times? And does Jesus really expect us to believe without having seen any evidence? Thomas points us toward some answers.

Poor Thomas! Because of this story, history has christened him "Doubting Thomas." We forget everything else about the man – he's immortalized as the one who didn't believe. Do we know that Thomas became a great missionary? According to old traditions, he preached the Gospel and planted churches as far away as India. Do we notice how courageous he was? On that Sunday evening the others had hidden themselves behind locked doors. Only Thomas was absent. Why? Was he the only one willing to leave their hideout to get some supplies or take care of some business? We also forget that Thomas spoke the clearest, most convincing, most complete confession of faith that ever came from this circle of disciples: "My Lord and My God!"

Perhaps most significantly, we forget that the other ten disciples need precisely the same thing that Thomas needs – visible, tangible reasons to believe. The resurrected Jesus walks in on them as they huddle behind locked doors. How do they react? They don't! (At least we don't read about any reaction.) "Peace be with you!" Jesus says. Still no reaction. Then he shows them his hands and his side. That's when they start rejoicing. Presumably, that is the point at which they first believe that the resurrected Jesus is really there.

Because we have a bias against Thomas, we are sure that faith must be independent of signs. And then it's impossible to take seriously the continuation of the text where John tells us that Jesus did many signs in the presence of his disciples – so many that John could only include a fraction of them in his Gospel. Not only that, but John, who wrote them down, was one of those hiding behind locked doors on that Easter Sunday evening. He was one of those who needed *yet another* sign before he could believe.

We forget all that, or maybe just skip over it, and say, "Thomas, Thomas! Why did you need signs? Why couldn't you just believe?"

We hear Jesus' words, "Blessed are those who have not seen and yet have believed," and forget that John himself didn't even belong to this group! He wasn't one of those who believed without seeing. He was one of those who had to see over and over again, and still had a hard time believing.

Just like we. We are no different than Jesus' disciples. In the celebrating, worshipping congregation we find it easier to believe. But how difficult it is to believe when we are alone, or full of fear, or in situations that appear hopeless.

Is it so bad if we find it hard to believe? Is it so bad if we want to *see?*

When we cast judgment on Thomas, we cast judgment on ourselves as well. We get into situations where we want to say, "If I don't see, if I don't feel, if I don't experience, then I can't believe!" What comes back to us is the accusing voice of our own conscience saying, "Shame on you for not being able to believe!" Moreover, we mistake that voice for Jesus or the voices of our fellow travelers on the road of faith. We don't know what to do with our doubts – feel guilty about them, defend them, or (worst of all) try to hide them.

How do we get out of this dilemma? I think we need to rehabilitate Thomas. I think we need to take a closer look at this text and see if it really says what we are accustomed to hearing.

We very easily make two mistakes when we interpret this text. The first is to understand Jesus' words, "Blessed are those who have not seen and yet believe," to mean, "Blessed are those who have absolutely no reason to believe, and believe anyway."

There is not a single hint anywhere in the Gospels that Jesus asked people to believe without having a reason to do so, as though faith could float in the air and never put roots into the realities of life. Jesus had performed many miraculous signs in the presence of his disciples. Why? So they could believe. In this text, Jesus first shows the ten disciples his hands. Why? So they can believe. Jesus shows Thomas his hands as well. Why? So he can believe. And John wrote all this down. Why? So we could believe.

Jesus does not demand a faith that has no reason to be there. In fact, God keeps offering people reasons to believe. He wants our faith to be based on something solid.

Then what does Jesus mean by, "Blessed are those who have not seen and yet have believed"? Could it mean, "Blessed are those who have not literally seen the resurrected Jesus but still find convincing reasons to believe"? Perhaps it means, "How blessed are those who find reasons to believe in the testimonies they hear, in the Scriptures they read, in the changed lives of others who have met Jesus – in the many different ways that God is at work in the community of faith and in the world."

This text is not about believing without reason to believe. Rather, it speaks to the value and need for convincing testimonies. Those who have experienced something bear witness to the presence and the work of Jesus, so that others can also know and have reason to believe. This text is about a faithfully preserved tradition, a convincingly preached word, a reliable Gospel record – a whole set of reasons for faith.

There is a second mistake we easily make when we hear Jesus' word: "Blessed are those who have not seen and yet have believed." We turn it around as though it means, "Cursed are those who don't believe unless they've seen for themselves." We automatically assume Jesus is scolding Thomas, and we feel just as scolded when our disbelief matches his.

If we met a starving man and gave him some bread, and then said to him, "Stop starving and eat!" would we be scolding? Or would we be providing what he needed and inviting an appropriate response? That, I think, is what Jesus is doing for Thomas. He is simply giving Thomas reason to believe, just as he had given the others.

Jesus is not scolding when he says, "Blessed are those who do not see and yet believe" – at least he isn't scolding *Thomas*. If anything there is a subtle admonition of the *other disciples* in Jesus' words.

Why wasn't Thomas able to believe? Why does Thomas have to experience again what the other ten had already experienced? Are they so unconvincing? Do they fail to give a believable testimony, fail to kindle sparks of faith in Thomas that they have indeed met the risen Lord?

Think about it. There are the disciples together with Thomas. The others claim that a week earlier, Jesus had come to them through locked doors. They claim that he encouraged them with the words, "Peace be with you!" They claim he had shown them his hands with the nail scars. "It had to be the Lord," they insist.

If you were Thomas, what would you ask? I would ask, "Then why are you still here hiding for fear of the Jews? Why aren't you out there proclaiming the good news?" If Thomas is having a hard time believing, maybe it isn't because he isn't good at believing. Maybe it is because the others aren't telling a convincing story.

Should we scold Thomas or sympathize with him? If you had been Thomas, would you have believed? Would you have believed an announcement that was supposed to be life-changing when the lives of those announcing it didn't seem changed?

"Blessed are those who have not seen and yet believe" doesn't mean, "Cursed are those who don't believe unless they have seen." It means something more like: "How blessed are those who live among people whose lives have been changed by meeting the resurrected Jesus. How blessed are those who are surrounded by credible witnesses, who hear believable testimonies. How blessed are those who live among people with a contagious faith, one that helps others find reasons to believe, even if they haven't personally experienced everything the others have."

This text is not so much about the *ability to believe*. It's more about *believability*. The ten are more in danger of judgment than Thomas is.

The ones who hear an admonishing word from Jesus are those who've experienced great things from God and then don't tell anyone about them. Or those who've had great experiences with God, and who report them enthusiastically, but then don't let these experiences have any effect on their lives. If Jesus scolds anyone, it is those who believe lots, but remain unbelievable themselves.

I think we've been unfair with Thomas. Sometimes we're unfair with ourselves as well. And not infrequently we're unfair with those among us who live in difficult situations and would love to believe, but just can't because the rest of us have a testimony that's too quiet or too unconvincing.

The call of this text is to be people on the lookout for reasons to believe, to be people who allow ourselves to be changed when those reasons come, to be people ready to share our experiences credibly with others who are still seeking reasons to believe. Next time we might be the ones who need the believable testimony of others to help build *our* faith. In this way we can walk together on the road of faith, on a road where we sometimes "see" but sometimes don't.

John, who wrote all this down for us, tells us that the signs were recorded "that you may believe ..." (20:30, 31; see next chapter).

John had seen a great deal. Then he passed on what he had seen to the readers of his Gospel. His goal was that others – even those who weren't there when the signs took place – would come to faith.

Was that a realistic hope? Sure it was! John became a believable witness. He allowed his life to be changed. Peter, too, reported that he had met the resurrected Lord, and expected other people to come to faith through his testimony. And they did! It was the same with Philip, and James, and Paul ... *and Thomas!* The disciples became credible witnesses. They allowed the resurrected Lord to change their lives, and many others came to faith on the basis of their testimony. These others found reason to believe in the changed lives of people who had seen and who then bore witness.

We, too, are sometimes privileged to see the great things God is doing in our day. At times we too can testify, "I have seen the Lord." And the more believably we can say that, the more visibly we let our experiences change our lives, the more effectively we will be able to help others whose faith is weak or who have never found a reason to believe. And next time, those we've helped might be doing the same for us.

Jesus and the Creeds

John 20:30,31

"Jesus did many other miraculous signs in the presence of his disciples, which are not recorded in this book. But these are written that you may believe that Jesus is the Christ, the Son of God, and that by believing you may have life in his name." (NIV)

This well-known text defines John's purpose in writing his Gospel. The signs which Jesus did led his disciples to believe and John records many of these so that future generations also will believe.

But what exactly are people supposed to believe on the basis of the "signs" and the "written record?" Most of us intuitively assume that John's purpose must be to establish what theologians call a "high Christology." While everyone knows that Jesus was a special person, not everyone believes that Jesus was truly sent by God, was the promised Messiah, was in fact God's very own Son. The Gospel is designed to lead people from a "low Christology" (Jesus was a special *human*) to a "high Christology" (Jesus was *God's Son*, indeed was himself *God*). That, at least, is what I always assumed John's Gospel aimed to do, and what John's "purpose statement" (20:30,31) verified.

What a great text this then becomes for systematic theologians. All we need to do is include a few verses from the context (the story of so-called "Doubting Thomas" precedes these verses), and we find a text that affirms both the death and resurrection of Jesus (central elements of every creed), and that highlights John's high Christology, again the central focus of most creeds and confessions. In this text, Jesus is confessed as *Lord* and as *God* by Thomas, and as *Christ* and *Son of God* by

John the writer. Clearly, these personal and Scriptural confessions point toward the orthodox creeds of the Christian church.

Moreover, the creeds of the church get another "shot in the arm" from this text and the Thomas story preceding it (at least as these are usually interpreted), for in them the reader is pointed away from direct *historical* and *experiential* bases for believing (after all, Thomas was apparently expected to believe without these). John 20 focuses on the centrality of *witness* (for Thomas was expected to believe on the basis of the other disciples' testimony) and even more clearly on the *still more central* basis for belief, *the Written Word*. "Blessed are those who have not seen and yet have believed" challenged Thomas to believe on the basis of apostolic testimony and continues to challenge John's readers to believe on the basis of the written record. "These things are *written*, that you might believe," says John. The Scriptures provide the data. Faith is the appropriate response. The creeds of the church capture the content. Systematic theology has a firm foundation.

This way of viewing the text (which I shall challenge in a minute!) seems to conform well to the theological preoccupations of many conservative theologians. The great enemy is liberalism; the great weapon is God's Word; the firm foundation for faith is the Christology of the early Christian creeds. This text, along with many others, contributes to our certainty that the orthodox faith of the church, which systematic theologians define and defend, is firmly grounded in Scripture. Nothing about the historical context of a given writer, the literary context of a particular text unit, *still less* the social context of the modern reader, are really relevant to a correct understanding of Scripture and its theological system. The Bible is unchanging and the truth it reveals is universal. We believe because ... well, because the Bible tells us *that* we must believe and *what* we must believe. That is one way of viewing things. It is not my way!

There is another way of thinking about theology and another way of interpreting John 20:30,31. Biblical theology (as opposed to systematic theology) is less concerned with universals and creeds. It is more concerned with particulars. It seeks the unique witness to truth expressed in any given text. It asks about the author's intentions, the historical circumstances of a book, and the literary context of any particular text unit. Even more significant, it asks each generation to read the text anew, seeking the particular biblical word that emerges when our situation is taken with us to the text and in turn challenged by it. The present value of a given text is not determined by which dogma it supports, but by how it resonates with issues that also need to be addressed today.

How would a biblical theologian look at John 20:30,31? I will not attempt to speak for others, but this is how I would look at it. First, I would not read it with one eye focused on the creeds of Nicea and Chalcedon. These did not exist when John wrote. John's direct aim was not to define or defend an orthodox and universal creed. While it is obvious that John's Gospel highlights the preexistent *Divine* Word, and points toward the authoritative *written* Word, it is even more centrally focused on the *particular* Word, the Word which was spoken by and "made flesh" in Jesus of Nazareth. According to John, this is the Word which calls and heals, redeems and changes lives.

Second, literary considerations would lead me to question whether this text is about believing without experiential evidence! The basis for Thomas' eventual belief was an experience of the resurrected Jesus. It would also have been the believable testimony of ten other disciples, if only they had been more credible (see preceding chapter on Thomas). According to John, people will come to believe when they hear the credible testimony of people whose lives have been changed by the resurrected Jesus. They will not come to faith just because some text or creed instructs them to believe.

If the Thomas story helps us discern *how* we can come to believe, the two verses following it (i.e. 20:30,31) center on *what* we should believe. The systematic theologian answers: John's "High Christology!" If only the liberals, the Jesus Seminar people for example, would do so, we could forget all this nonsense about Jesus being just a great human who somehow revealed God!

I suggested above that I was about to challenge the traditional reading of these verses. Here goes. This text, I propose, challenges the orthodox faith of conservatives at least as directly as the heresies of the liberals – perhaps even more directly. The reason we usually think this text is about defining a high Christology is that we have one eye on the dangers of liberalism and the other on the creeds of the church. No wonder we find in this text what we want to find.

Every modern version of John 20:31 that I am aware of reads, "These are written that you might believe that Jesus is the Christ, the

Son of God." We assume that this means Jesus' identity is being defined in ever more exalted terms. He is not only Jesus (the human), not only the Christ (the promised Messiah), he is indeed God's very own Son. Now, don't get me wrong. I am not calling these doctrines into question. What I call into question is whether these points are really the focus of these verses. Perhaps they should be read differently.

There is a more likely alternative reading. Greek sentences containing both a subject and a predicate nominative (a complement) are often (unlike English) hard to interpret. In English we can distinguish between the phrases "God is love" and "Love is God" because the words are in a different order. In Greek, word order alone is not an adequate guide as to which word in a sentence is the subject. So authors used subtle signals, like dropping articles and locating complements immediately before the "to be" verb, in order to help readers figure out which is the subject and which is the complement.

When we debate with Jehovah's Witnesses about the correct translation of John 1:1, we argue tooth and nail that the Greek complement rule justifies our translation "The Word was God" rather than "God was the Word" or "The Word was a god" (and the rules of Greek grammar support our claim). However, the same rules, when applied to John 20:31, suggest that John did not want to say: "These are written that you might believe that Jesus is the Christ, the Son of God." Rather he wanted to say, "These are written that you might believe that the Christ, the Son of God, is Jesus." Or, if we want to preserve the usual word order, we might translate it: "These are written that you might believe that *Jesus* (and no one else) is the Christ, the Son of God."

Perhaps that does not seem like a significant revision. Yet the difference is rather important. Translated the usual way, John is claiming his book was written to define and defend a high Christology. Jesus was not merely a human, he was more. He was Messiah; indeed he was Son of God; indeed he was very God of very God – therefore the creeds are true, the Jesus Seminar scholars are wrong; orthodoxy is saved!

Turning the sentence around (as I believe John intended), John's Gospel has a different goal. John's theological opponents were not the Greek ontologists of the 4th century, nor the historians of the Jesus Seminar. His theological opponents believed in many christs and many divine sons and daughters. In John's religious environment there were many religious leaders promising liberation from slavery and oppression, from sin and guilt, or from meaninglessness and fear of death. His world was populated with many would-be messiahs! And there were also many divine visitors, sons and daughters of the gods, filling up the mythological *pleroma* between heaven and earth, semi-divine beings that mediated between the spiritual and the physical.

John's Gospel says: "No!" John's Gospel says that *the* Messiah, the only one who can deliver ... *the* Son of God, the only one who truly reveals God ... is *Jesus*, Jesus of Nazareth, a concrete person who did the works of God, spoke the words of God, and showed by his faithful life what pleases God, Jesus of Nazareth who died and rose again to redeem us back to God. The deliverer and revelation of God is no semi-divine being who made a guest appearance on earth. He was truly human, a particular human, Jesus! John writes his Gospel in order that, by believing, we might have life in *his* name, not in anyone else's name, but in *his* name!

And if John had this agenda in mind, no wonder he insisted in the prologue "the Word became *flesh* (i.e. a human person)." His opponents did not need to be persuaded that the one who became flesh was indeed the Word, but rather that the one who was the Word did indeed become *Flesh*.

John 20:30,31 does not critique the *naturalism* of the liberals as much as it critiques their *pluralism*! And even though the low Christology of many liberals needs to be critiqued, this text really critiques the theology of many conservatives. Too often conservatives affirm a high Christology, but do not really believe in the true humanity of Jesus, nor understand the significance of his human life, his ministry, his modeling. I suggest this text confronts the heresy of those who affirm historical creeds, but do not recognize that even more central to biblical faith than fourth century creeds is a community of faithful disciples, bearing a credible witness to the significance of Jesus of Nazareth who lived and served among us to reveal the Father, and who died and rose again to reconcile us to God.

In John's letters, John argues that anyone denying that Jesus Christ is come "in the flesh" is not of God. Many theologians fight to defend a high Christology, and have virtually no room in their theology for the human Jesus, for the one John describes as the one "we have looked upon, and our hands have handled." When John wrote, it was the *real humanity* of Jesus that was in danger of being forgotten. He lived in an age that was impressed with all sorts of "saviors and lords," all sorts of "messiahs" and "divine sons." John's goal was not to prove that the human Jesus was in fact the divine Word. It was to prove that the divine Word *actually became flesh and dwelt among us in a specific concrete person, Jesus of Nazareth.*

This text was written to challenge pluralists ("there are many ways to God") and docetists ("Jesus only seemed human") and Gnostics ("a truly divine person could not also be human") – people who needed to be convinced that the Savior of the world was one into whose side a hand could be thrust, in whose hands nail holes could be seen and felt, one who could eat, one who could speak peace, one who could change scared followers into a community of courageous disciples and missionaries.

It's an amazing thing that precisely when we take the original context of these verses seriously, they turn out to be *very relevant* to our own age, more relevant (I propose) than if they function only to define and defend the classical creeds.

We are moving into a very spiritual age, where spirit guides and even angels play all sorts of ambiguous roles, roles that approximate those of mediator and Savior. And at the same time we live in a very secular age where the "messiahs" that promise to deliver us from evil are sometimes political, sometimes economic, sometimes military, sometimes academic.

The witness of John is that only one can deliver, only one can bridge the chasm between God and humanity, and that is Jesus, the true flesh and blood Jesus who lived and died and rose again.

Some people's Christology is indeed too low. But this text challenges those whose Christology is too docetic, too nebulous, not firmly centered in Jesus of Nazareth.

The major contribution of this particular text is not to help define and defend the high Christology of the creeds. Indeed it needs to be set free from those shackles, so that it might speak a powerful word to those who come to it with modern and post-modern questions. If we stop filtering texts through the creeds, we find in them all sorts of echoes and themes and paradigms and claims that resonate with our needs.

The *Big* Miracle in Philippi

Acts 16:6-40

Sometimes the biggest miracles of all are those that we don't even realize are miracles – until our eyes are opened. And when we see them, we can do nothing but marvel! And sometimes the best stories are told in such a way that the most astonishing part is at least partially hidden between the lines, but just waiting to be found. Here's how I think Luke expected us to read the narrative we find recorded in Acts 16.

Paul was tired of having his plans changed. He had sketched out this whole missionary trip in detail. First, he would re-visit the churches he had planted earlier, strengthening, encouraging and organizing them. Then he would head further into Asia Minor and Bythinia. That would allow the momentum of the Gospel in the region to expand gradually to the neighboring cities. It was the only plan that made sense to him. But nothing was working out!

Wherever the missionaries turned, they ran into roadblocks. Could this be God redirecting them to territories not yet targeted? What was God up to, anyway? Luke tells the story like this:

> Paul and his companions traveled throughout the region of Phrygia and Galatia, having been kept by the Holy Spirit from preaching the word in the province of Asia. When they came to the border of Mysia, they tried to enter Bithynia, but the Spirit of Jesus would not allow them to. So they passed by Mysia and went down to Troas. During the night Paul had a vision of a man of Macedonia standing and begging him, "Come over to Macedonia and help us."

- The Holy Spirit said this.
- The Spirit of Jesus didn't let them.
- And then comes the vision of a man across the sea calling for help.

Somehow God wanted to make it very clear: the missionary movement into Macedonia was not a matter of human planning and strategic decisions. It was something God had planned and something God made happen. And when God intervenes that persistently, God must be up to something.

The missionaries Paul and Silas, with a few companions, headed across the Aegean Sea. Well, guess what? There was no man standing on the shore, waiting for Paul, anticipating his help. At least, no one Paul could see.

In fact, Paul searched in vain for a Jewish synagogue. There was none. No natural springboard for a ministry of Gospel proclamation. And what's more, Paul knew what it meant that there was no synagogue. It meant there were fewer than ten Jewish men in the entire city. That was the condition for the founding of a synagogue: there had to be ten Jewish men – only nine Jewish men, even if there were one hundred women as well, still fell one short of the minimum number.

What to do now? No man on the beach waiting for Paul's help. No synagogue as a springboard for their missionary proclamation. But Paul was resourceful, and he knew the ways of the Jews. All he had to do was wait for the Sabbath, and he would find those who worshipped the God of Israel. Lacking a synagogue, they would gather at the riverbank, temporarily turning it into a place of prayer.

Sabbath arrived. Paul and his companion Silas made their way to the riverside. But still no Jewish men showed up. Not even one who might qualify as the man in Paul's vision! Only a few women, among them a wealthy businesswoman named Lydia. We now shift to her side of the story.

The first transformation

Lydia was not a native of Philippi. A good guess is that she had followed her husband to Philippi where business opportunities had opened up. But he had since died, and she now ran both the household and a thriving business. Life had treated her well in her adopted home. She was wealthy. She was respected. And, though there was no synagogue to attend, she did continue to worship the God of the Jews in fellowship with a few other women.

A surprise awaited her on this particular Sabbath, as she arrived at the usual place of prayer. A group of men were there, conversing with the women who had arrived before her. This day had started out like any other Sabbath. But it turned out to be a day that would change Lydia's life forever. She would still be managing her household and her business. But nothing would be the same after today!

Something touched Lydia deeply as she heard Paul preach, and she responded with an open heart, "I believe!" And before the day was over, she was baptized along with others in her household. She had become a follower of the Jesus way – indeed, she had become the very first convert through missionary preaching on European soil. Now *that* is a miracle! But as I hinted earlier, I think Luke is setting us up to ponder a miracle more remarkable still, before this chapter is over.

I suspect that when Lydia retired for the night on that special Sabbath evening, she said to herself: "Who would ever have imagined that I'd experience what happened today." Little did she know that she'd be saying those words again soon, in response to a miracle more remarkable still!

Luke temporarily leaves the Lydia story to narrate two other conversions. But he will come back to Lydia later, and so will we.

Two more tranformations

The second transformation story in Acts 16 involves a new set of characters. These were not pious women worshipping the God of Israel. These were ruthless men exploiting a slave girl. And the girl was no Lydia, well respected, wealthy, influential, worshipper of God. On the contrary, she was a Macedonian – a demented Macedonian – an enslaved demented Macedonian – wracked by demons, enslaved by unscrupulous men taking advantage of her occult abilities for their personal gain. Paul was not particularly impressed, as the demonic spirit in this girl provided unwanted publicity for his missionary preaching. He turned around in irritation and demanded that the demon leave. It did and she was healed – another miracle chocked up in this amazing chapter. And I am going to make the educated guess that her conversion is the next miracle.

Neither of these miracles particularly impressed her exploiters. They were furious. And they turned their anger on Paul and Silas. Soon the missionaries, who had delivered a poor slave girl from her bondage, experienced bondage themselves. They were accosted, falsely charged, stripped, beaten and finally thrown into the local jail. The rest of the story is, I think, quite well known. The missionaries were praising the Lord, singing songs of joy at midnight. Suddenly God sent an earthquake. The prison cells were torn open. Paul and Silas somehow persuaded all the prisoners to sit tight and wait for the jailer to secure them again. Now I don't know how many miracles to count in this short narrative. At the very least a well-timed earthquake, though perhaps one could count the midnight duet in circumstances like this as a miracle as well. And what about Paul's ability to keep all the freshly released prisoners together?

But Luke moves quickly to the next miracle, the conversion of the Philippian jailer and his household. I suppose the jailer had to account somehow for all the miracles he has just witnessed. At any rate he positively begged the missionaries to explain to him the way of salvation, before they even started their evangelistic preaching.

A miraculous beginning

There we have it – three conversion stories, three individuals highlighted, their lives radically changed by the Gospel. In fact, one is almost tempted to consider Lydia's transformation the least spectacular of them all. She had already worshipped the God of Israel. She had already been a fine upstanding lady, well-respected, influential. So now she also believes in Jesus. A transformation to be sure, but think of the slave girl.

Nothing is the same for her! She is psychologically healed, spiritually delivered, socially restored. I suppose she had always been somehow interested in spiritual things, but now she sees everything from the other side. Not demons, but the Spirit of the living God has invaded her life. She is a free woman again, free to find a new life as a follower of Jesus.

And think of the jailer. He was a prison guard, perhaps with little or no interest in spiritual things, maybe a brutal man, no doubt a Roman. In the middle of the night, everything changes. Now he is a follower of the Prince of Peace. Just as Lydia had done, he opens his home to the missionaries and they fellowship together. And just like Lydia, he brings his entire household with him into this embryonic Christian community.

Three conversion stories; three lives transformed. But maybe for all three, and especially for Lydia, the greatest transformation was still coming! Perhaps the evening when she would go to rest and say, "Who would ever have thought it?" still lay ahead.

Luke is an amazing storyteller. He could easily have told Lydia's story, then the story of the slave girl, then the one about the prison guard, *and then simply moved on to other things*. But he doesn't. Before the chapter is over Lydia is revisited, not only by the missionaries, but by Luke the storyteller. You see, Luke is not quite finished with his litany of miracles in Acts 16.

The adventures of the missionary team take an interesting turn when the magistrates of the city decide to release the prisoners and expel them from the city. So they make their way to the jail to order their release, never suspecting that the missionaries have spent the night fellowshipping and feasting with the jailer.

Feisty Paul, however, is not willing to be shushed out of the city. He accuses the officials of mishandling a Roman citizen, and boldly re-enters the city. And that sets the stage for the final miracle.

The last verse of this long chapter reads like this: "After Paul and Silas came out of prison, they went to Lydia's house, *where they met with the believers*, and encouraged them. Then they left."

So what is Luke inviting us to read between the lines? Well first, who exactly are these believers whom Paul encouraged, as they gathered together for one last visit with the missionaries in Lydia's home? Well, we've just heard their stories, haven't we?

- An upper-class God-fearing well-respected Jewish business-woman;
- a demented, psychologically damaged, exploited Macedonian slave girl;
- and a non-religious, brutal, Roman prison guard.

Only now all three have become believers.

If you were going to plant a church, how would you feel about a core group like this? Three nationalities, three social classes, three kinds of religious background, two women and one man. Paul, you sure know how to put together a core group for a church plant!

The Jews played it safe – ten Jewish men; not one less would do. That way there is momentum, there is a clear direction, a strong tradition. Paul was crazy enough simply to believe Jesus. Where two or three are gathered together in Jesus' name, there he is present, there is church.

Is there anything else Luke wants us to read between the lines? I think so! Did you notice the hospitality theme woven through this chapter? Lydia obviously felt quite honored the first time the missionaries graced her home. Her invitation was: "If you consider me a believer in the Lord, come and stay at my house."

And I suspect it was an unforgettable moment for both the jailer and the missionaries when he escorted them out of their jail cell, washed their wounds, led them right into his own home and set a fellowship meal before them in the middle of the night.

But the high point of the chapter, of the entire story, of this litany of miracles, is not reached in the conversion stories of these three, nor in the hospitality extended to the missionaries by their converts. The high point comes in the last verse – when all the believers gather in Lydia's house!

I suspect that Paul politely invited himself and his fellow missionaries over for a farewell dinner, and then added provocatively: P.S. "Guess who's coming for dinner?"

I suspect that it was on *that* evening, more than on any other, that Lydia laid her head to rest and thought back over that amazing day, repeating over and over in her mind and spirit: "Who would have thought it? Who could ever have imagined it?"

Are you picturing it? Here is how I imagine it: At one end of the table sits a wealthy, upstanding, Jewish businesswoman. On her left is a brutal, middle-class, Roman prison guard (at least that is what he was last week). Next to him is a demented, Macedonian slave girl (at least that is what she was a week ago). Then come the missionaries, and the circle is complete. Now they are brothers and sisters, sharing a family meal. There is only one power in all the world sufficient to draw precisely this group together and transform it into a family. Only the Gospel can do that!

When Lydia invited the rabbi Paul to join her for a meal on that first Sabbath evening, could she ever in her wildest imagination have dreamed that it would come to this? This day, the day of the farewell fellowship meal, would stand out in Lydia's mind for the rest of her life as the day she knew beyond all doubt: Life would never be the same again!

Three totally diverse people have become brothers and sisters. And as they gather in Jesus' name, Jesus is among them. Precisely in order to bring about *this miracle*, God pushed, and diverted, and coaxed the missionaries until they arrived in Philippi. And then God used them to gather the participants for this final dramatic scene.

Who would have believed it?

So who was the man from Macedonia in Paul's vision? Who was standing on the other side of the Aegean saying, "Come over and help"? Interpreters have tried various suggestions. I think Luke was thinking of none other than Jesus! In Luke's view, Jesus was guiding and directing and pushing and pulling the missionaries all the way to Troas. And then Jesus, who had already been there ahead of the missionaries, called from across the sea: "Hey, Paul, I'm planning a miracle – a *big* miracle. Can you please come over and help me?" What miracle? The conversion of Lydia? Sure. The deliverance of a slave girl? Yes, indeed. The conversion of the Philippian jailer? Yes, that, too. But the biggest miracle Jesus did was to take these three people and bring them together around Lydia's dining room table, to eat their family meal and tell the missionaries: "Bye guys, we can take it from here on!"

Does any of this have anything to say to us? Well, just as Luke invited us to read between his lines, I trust you have also been reading between mine. And I trust that God will do such a magnificent miracle in us, that we too will soon find ourselves lying in bed and reminiscing:

- reflecting on the diverse group of people that we call brothers and sisters;
- marveling at the wide array of people with whom we worship;
- calling to mind who has gathered in the family circle around our dining table;

... and then saying: "Who would ever have thought it? Who in their wildest imagination could ever have believed this would be possible?"

Working Together for Good

Romans 8:28

And we know that all things work together for good to them that love God, to them who are the called according to his purpose. (KJV)

That is how I once memorized Romans 8:28 many years ago. It has often been a word of hope for me, assuring me that all things, even "bad" things, will turn out "for good" to those who love God. In fact there was a time when I interpreted this verse to mean that there really are no "bad things" that happen to believers. If things seem bad, but really serve to fulfill God's good purposes for us, then even these things are ultimately good. I guess at the time it did not seem unjust to me that only those who love God are promised the benefit of "everything working out." Nor was I troubled by the fact that I often did not see the "bad things" magically transformed into "good things."

I have undergone two changes of mind in my understanding of this verse. I want to share these.

The first (minor) adjustment in my understanding of Romans 8:28 happened when I realized that modern versions of the Bible translate it differently at a very crucial point. In the NIV (for example) the verse does not say that "all things work together" (as though there is some deep magic in the universe that somehow creates the hidden "good" pattern out of all the "bad" pieces). Rather it says, "In all things, *God* works for the good of those who love him." This version attributes the "working out" not to some universal magic, but directly to God's active involvement.

Now that I am able to read the verse in the original language, I know what caused the change from the KJV to the NIV. The KJV translators viewed *"panta"* (all things) as the *subject* of the verb *"sunergei"* (work together). The NIV translators view *"panta"* (all things) as the *object* of the verb.

Both versions (i.e. with *panta* as subject or as object) are grammatically possible in Greek. For those who care about such things, this results from two facts: first, the word *panta* has the same form whether it is used as subject or object; second, the word *panta*, though plural, can be used with a singular verb. However, though both versions, KJV and NIV, are grammatically possible, the NIV version is to be preferred for two reasons:

- Linguistically: The Greek word *sunergei* (from which the English word "synergy" comes) does not mean "work out" or "fall in place." In the New Testament, it always signifies the active involvement of real actors accomplishing some task. To treat *"panta"* as the subject implies that *everything that happens* is actively and consciously working at the project of making good things happen to people who love God. That kind of claim would be linguistically odd, to say the least.

- Theologically: The Scriptures never attribute good will and active working to "all things." If good things are being made to happen, it is because *God* is at work, transforming "all things" into something they would not become on their own.

Thus, the NIV translation: "In *all things*, God works for the good of those who love him" is clearly better than the KJV translation, "All things work together for good to those who love God."

Now, if you were to check an NIV Bible (preferably an older edition), you might see an interesting (though slightly misleading) footnote. That footnote alludes to the two ways of translating the text indicated above. It also indicates (correctly) that a small number of ancient manuscripts include two words in Romans 8:28 which are absent in most manuscripts and were not taken into account by the KJV translators. Those words are *"ho theos"* (i.e. "God" used as a subject). If those words were original, we would have no choice but to declare the NIV right and the KJV wrong about which is the subject of the verb. As it is, we need to make a judgment call, and based on both linguistic and theological considerations, the NIV is judged far more likely than the KJV. The NIV footnote is misleading if we understand it to say that the NIV translation depends on the inclusion of these two words. In reality, the NIV translation is better, even though these two words do not belong to the text. It is not unlikely that an early scribe, recognizing that the text could be interpreted two ways, slipped in the extra words to make sure that the text was understood correctly (i.e. the way we now read it in the NIV).

If that was too complicated, let me try once more: the NIV footnote correctly notes that some manuscripts do and some do not explicitly say that God is the subject of the verb. And it also correctly indicates that the verse can be translated two ways. But it wrongly implies that if the words "*ho theos*" are not considered original, then the verse should be translated as in the KJV.

To summarize: I once thought Romans 8:28 was about "all things working out" and am now persuaded it is about "God working for good in all situations."

Now to the second time I changed my understanding of this verse. Even the translation that is given in the NIV needs to be reconsidered. The biggest problem with the NIV version is that it still misunderstands what the verb *sunergei* ("work together") really means. The NIV translation, though correctly viewing God as the subject, incorrectly represents what God is doing. It treats *sunergei* as though it means God is "working things together" i.e. "forming a pattern" or "mixing ingredients together" so that something new, i.e. something good, emerges. *Sunergei* in Greek is not about one party working various ingredients together; it is about *more than one party* "working together" on a common project. It means, quite literally, "work together." If Romans 8:28 says that God "works together", then the appropriate question is not, "*What* does God work together?" The appropriate question is, "*With whom* does God work together?" If we read the text differently, the answer is clearly supplied in Romans 8:28.

I have before me a new edition of the NIV. It contains *two* footnotes to this verse. The first is the same as the one contained in the older version (discussed above). The second says this: "or ... works together with those who love him to bring about what is good ... " This way of reading the verse still views "God" as the subject of the verb "works together." However, on this reading "those who love God" are not the *beneficiaries* of God's interventions; they are God's *co-workers*! Romans 8:28 is not about God working to bring about good things for us (though God also does that). Romans 8:28 is about God working *with us* to bring about good things in *all situations* (reading *panta* now not as the direct object of the verb, but as an accusative of reference.)

Those who have studied Greek know that the dative case can be used (among other possibilities) as a "dative of advantage" or as an "instrument of association." The traditional reading of Romans 8:28 takes the phrase "those who love God" in the first way (God works "for us" that is, "for our advantage"). The NIV second footnote interprets it the second way (God works "with us" that is, "alongside of us"). Both are grammatically possible. So how does one decide which is correct?

The best way is to look again at the verb *sunergei*. Is it used in Scripture to speak of making things fit together / fall in place / produce a pattern? Or is it used to speka of two parties that are working as a team? In all four other occurrences of this word in the New Testament, it has the latter meaning (cf. Mark 16:20; 1 Cor. 16:16; 2 Cor. 6:1; James 2:22.) Of these, the first three speak explicitly of God working with people or people working with each other. In the fourth, "faith and works" are viewed metaphorically as two parties "working along with each other." The only way that *sunergei* is used in the New Testament is when there are two or more parties "working together." Moreover, the noun associated with this verb (*sunergos* i.e. co-worker, helper, fellow worker) is also always used to represent two or more parties that are working along with each other! (cf. Rom. 16:3, 9, 21; 1 Cor. 3:9; 2 Cor. 1:24; 8:23; Phil. 2:25; 4:3; Col. 4:11; 1 Thess. 3:2; Philemon 24; 2 John 8). Thus the word is not about making *things* work together; it is about *two parties* working together.

Romans 8:28 is not about God fitting all things together into a pattern for our benefit. It is about God and those who love God working as partners, "working together" to bring about good in all situations. While we (i.e. those who love God and are called according to God's purposes) may at times also be the *beneficiaries* of "God and others" working together, this verse is not about that. It is not about the benefits we receive from God's action on our behalf. It is rather a call to those who have been "foreknown, predestined, called, justified and glorified" (see the context of Romans 8:28) to be not only *recipients* of

God's grace, but also *channels* of God's grace to others. We were called by God; we love God; and thus we join God's work in the world. God is working to bring about good, and we are God's fellow-workers. God's good purposes will often come about in terrible situations, not because someone "sat back and trusted God's promise" but because someone "joined God's work in the world, became God's hands and feet, became a tangible expression of God's love and caring."

Romans 8:28 is a challenge for us to be those sorts of people. If we are, then ever more people will learn that nothing can separate them from God's love (see the context of Romans 8:28). Wherever and whenever they feel separated from God's love, God is sending co-workers; God is sending us, to assure them in concrete and tangible ways that God still loves them. That is, at any rate, the way I think Romans 8:28 should be interpreted.

Yet, having said all this, I must confess that it is hard to say farewell to an older interpretation that has been with me since childhood and has comforted and encouraged me in difficult times. Must I abandon my earlier view in order to accept my newer insights? Not necessarily.

Another possibility remains open. Sometimes a sentence in the Bible is "deliberately ambiguous" (technically it is called polyvalent). Two (or more) options are grammatically possible and *both* (or more than two) meanings are intended by the author. Perhaps this is one of those situations. I doubt that the *usual* readings of the KVJ and the NIV are both correct. There I think we need to make a choice. But I am less sure that we need to make a choice between the NIV reading and the one suggested in the NIV's second footnote. Perhaps this verse is about God working both *with* us and *for* us to bring about good in tough situations. (For Greek students, this might mean the dative is a dative of reference.) This understanding would portray the Christian community as a fellowship of "grace-recipients" and at the same time "grace-givers." God along with God's co-workers (our brothers and sisters) have been instrumental in "bringing about good things" in our lives; now we join God and God's other co-workers, helping to bring about good things in the lives of others.

This way of reading Romans 8:28 coheres well with the broader context of the verse in Romans 8. There we learn that God has not yet made everything turn out for good. That is why all creation, including God's own children, still groan, waiting for their final redemption (cf.

vv. 18-27). And that is why, in every imaginable difficulty, we can be assured that God's love never leaves us (cf. vv. 31-39). The community of those being transformed by God (cf. vv. 29,30) first receives God's grace and then passes it on as we "work with God" to bring about what is good.

It is hard to preach a text that has a meaning (or multiple meanings) not clearly captured in the Bible translations most people carry. But at least those who have new NIV Bibles can find an alternative reading of Romans 8:28 in a footnote. It is my hope that this alternative reading soon finds its way into more translations. Then Romans 8:28 can challenge us (as I believe Paul intended) to be God's co-workers, instruments of God's loving care to others, inside and outside the community of faith.

Praising the Lord Who Blesses Us

Ephesians 1:3

S ometimes praises flow from us like laughter from delighted children. When we feel God's presence, when we recognize God's help and encouragement, when we hear good news and we just *know* God is blessing us ... *then* we effortlessly praise.

But how do we deal with verses in Scripture that call us to praise God even when things *aren't* going well, verses that call us to be thankful and filled with praise in *all kinds* of situations? Consider Habakkuk 3:17,18:

> Though the fig tree does not bud, and there are no grapes on the vines; though the olive crop fails and the fields produce no food; though there are no sheep in the pen and no cattle in the stalls, yet I will rejoice in the LORD; I will be joyful in God my Savior.

Can we also say in *these* circumstances, "Yes! That is what I'll do"? Or are we inclined to respond more like: "How can that be possible? How can it be genuine? When everything is going wrong, this kind of exuberant praise is just a pretence, isn't it? It's going through the motions or words of praise, but *can't* genuinely come from the heart."

Yet some say the only way to guarantee God's blessing is to offer our praises while things look awful. There are theories – even some popular books – that teach that when we hear bad news, when everything is going wrong, *that's* when we must give praises to God. If we do, then we can expect God to somehow change the bad news into good news, or our difficult situations into blessed miracles.

There was a time when I gobbled up those books. How wonderful! All we have to do is speak out our praises to God and God will turn all our problems into great blessings. I remember a number of situations in which I, and some of my friends, took this very seriously; perhaps we even overdid it just a bit – like the time we caused a traffic accident with our old Ford Econoline van. We climbed out of the van and before we even attempted to converse with the other driver, we took our guitar out of the vehicle and sang with great enthusiasm, right out in the middle of the street: "Praise ye the Lord, Halleluia!" Of course, the other driver thought we were completely crazy, and I'm not so sure anymore that he was wrong.

We thought if we praised enthusiastically enough, God would have to turn the event into a blessing. Is this what it means to praise the Lord in all situations? Is this the motivation?

Ephesians 1:3 speaks directly to this matter of how and when and why we praise God:

> Praise be to the God and Father of our Lord Jesus Christ, who has blessed us in the heavenly realms with every spiritual blessing in Christ.

I want to pose three questions of this text, and suggest answers that help us understand this important and, as we shall discover, surprising verse.

- What do we mean when we talk about "praising God"?
- What is the relationship between our praise to God and God's blessing us?
- What does it mean to speak of God "blessing us"?

What does it mean to "praise God"?

Paul uses a word in this verse that's actually pretty easy to understand, even for English speakers. The word is *eulogetos*. Does that sound a bit like an English word you know? *Eulogy*. It's a speech that says nice things about someone. We often use them at funerals when it wouldn't be right to speak badly of the person we're remembering. And that's exactly what *eulogetos* means in Greek. It is speaking words of affirmation, words of acclamation, words that recount the good things a person has done.

There is an even more common word in English that means the same thing: *"praise."* When we praise people, we speak well of them. You don't have to know Greek to remember that the word translated "praise" in this text actually means "praise"! We praise God when we speak of God's greatness, God's goodness, God's mercy, holiness, and power. The word means the same thing when we apply it to people. We praise someone by concentrating on his/her good points. It doesn't mean we can't find any faults. It means we don't concentrate on them. We praise. We speak well of.

What is the relationship between our praise to God and God blessing us?

Ephesians 1:3 is pretty clear about this: *We praise God because God has blessed us.* We don't praise so we can squeeze a blessing out of God. We praise because we recognize the blessing has already been given. God takes the first step; our praise is the response. Of course, this sequence works only if we *recognize* that the blessings we experience are gifts from God.

What does it mean for God to bless us?

This is the toughest of the questions. I remember the prayers I learned to pray as a child: "Dear God, bless mom and dad, bless grandma and grandpa, bless Ron and Wes and Larry and Ken and Donna, bless all the missionaries in the whole world." I didn't have a clue what I really wanted for these people; I just wanted God to bless them.

Usually we imagine that a blessing from God is something good we want done for us. We say we are blessed when we experience good times, good things, good relationships, good success.

A blessing would be safety when we travel, health, prosperity, all the things we would love to experience on a regular basis. And so we understand the relationship between praising God and experiencing blessings in accordance with this. God gives us *things, good things,* and we give God praise: words of appreciation and affirmation. We realize how rich we are, how well things are going, how many things we enjoy, and as a result we praise our God who has been so generous.

If this is how we do it, it isn't hard to figure out why we run into problems. What do we do when we *don't* feel rich, when things *aren't* going well, when we're *not* enjoying our circumstances? We stop praising

God. If health is a blessing, what is sickness? If good relationships are a blessing, what are difficult ones? If they're not blessings, what happens to our praise?

Here is where we need to come back to Ephesians 1:3 and to the surprise I promised we would find. According to Ephesians 1:3, our praise to God is not connected to the good *things* that God gives us. It is connected to something else. The word "blessing" or "blessed" means something altogether different in this verse than safety and health and riches and good relationships.

It is a word connected to what Solomon spoke of when he wrote this proverb:

> A good name is more desirable than great riches; to be esteemed is better than silver or gold. (Proverbs 22:1)

According to Solomon in Proverbs 22:1, and also according to Paul in the text we are examining, the great blessing to be celebrated, a blessing greater than any kind of riches, is the blessing of a good reputation. Being *well-spoken of* is what really counts; that is what gives us something to praise God about. A good reputation is worth more than houses and lands, silver and gold, health and wealth, family and friends.

I can already hear the protests: "That's even worse!! That's great for people with a good reputation, but I'm not one of them! If I have to wait until my reputation is great, I'll praise God less than if I link my praise to health, wealth and happiness. If a good reputation is what elicits praise, I might as well give up now."

And that is where we're wrong! Ephesians 1:3 is not about a good reputation with our fellow human beings, our friends and families, churches, colleagues. It's not about what humans are thinking or saying about us. It's about our reputation with God. Every one of us who has said "Yes" to God through Jesus Christ has a good reputation with God. Everyone.

Listen to how God thinks of us:

> I have called you by name, you are mine. (Isaiah 43:1)

> I summon you by name and bestow on you a title of honor. (Isaiah 45:4)

To all who believe in his name, he gave the right to become children of God. (John 1:12)

How great is the love the Father has lavished on us, that we should be called children of God! And that is what we are! (1 John 3:1)

I no longer call you servants, but I call you friends. (John 15:15)

That is what God says about us – about all who say "yes" to God through Jesus. Not just about those who are active in church work or those who are spiritually mature – not just those who have a great reputation in the church or in society. Through Jesus Christ, every believer has a great reputation with God. God speaks well of us. We are given names of honor.

Now for the surprise. Let's read Ephesians 1:3 again, but this time translated word for word from the original language.

May the God and Father of our Lord Jesus Christ be well-spoken of, who has spoken well of us, with a spiritual eulogy, in the heavenlies, in Christ.

Most translations say, "Praise be to God" where the text talks about being well-spoken of. This is appropriate because praising actually means speaking good things about someone. But the second time Paul uses the very same word, the translations change it to "blessed," as though Paul is now talking about something else. But Paul didn't change words! In fact, though he had to change the form in order to fit the grammar of his sentence, he actually took the same word and used it three times: once for what we do to God, once for what God has already done to us, and then again to describe that which we experience because of our connection with Jesus Christ. In all three places, Paul uses the word from which we get the English word "eulogy." In other words:

May the God and Father of our Lord Jesus Christ be eulogized (may God be well-spoken of – *eulogetos*), who has eulogized us (who has already spoken well of us – eulogesas) with every possible eulogy (*eulogia*) in the heavenlies in Christ.

Paul used the same word three times. Paul didn't want our praise to be linked to the "stuff" God gives us. He wanted it linked to the words of praise coming from God's own mouth about us, God's children. And so we would do well to translate the same word the same way:

Praise God who has praised us; or

Blessed be God, who has blessed us; or, more literally,

May good words be spoken about God, who has spoken good words about us!

Then we would capture the reciprocal relationship that Paul is describing here.

We don't praise God first and foremost for health and wealth and happiness, for safety and friends and personal success. We praise God because of what God says about us in Jesus Christ. God has spoken well of us, and we therefore speak well of God. God speaks in our defense, and we speak in God's.

When people criticize us, God says of us, "To me you are precious, you have a name of honor, I call you friend." When people criticize God, we say in response, "To us God is precious, God's name is honored, God is my friend."

This verse is about a friendship, a mutual relationship, a partnership of loyalty and love and the words of appreciation and affirmation that go with it. If we are God's children, God sticks by us, even if we don't always live up to our calling. God sticks up for us, even though our lives often don't merit God's favor. God speaks well of us, not because we deserve it, but because we are seated in the heavenlies with Christ.

And in response, we stick by God, stick up for God, we speak well of God – not because we are given all that we want, but because we are joined with God in the heavenlies in Christ.

That is the basis of our praise! Though good things may remind us of God's favor towards us, we don't praise God for the good things; we praise because we are intimately connected in a relationship of loyalty, love and friendship. Though tough times may come our way, we can praise God because whatever our circumstances, God loves and accepts us fully through Jesus.

Maybe that sounds strange – God and us, praising each other, sticking up for each other, speaking well of each other. But that's what Paul is talking about here, and it's all possible if we're prepared to accept that *true* blessing from God is not measured in the things valued in this life, but in the spiritual blessings available through Christ.

And when we are clear about that, we can praise God when the morning is beautiful and when we tire of the rain, when we experience good health and when we struggle with illness, when the crops are plentiful and when they are scarce, in good times and bad, knowing that even death cannot separate us from the one who speaks well of us, no matter what anyone else says.

We Prayed for Healing...
But She Died

James 5:14-18

We were sure God had promised healing; we thought that meant the cancer would not come back. But it did. We prayed for healing. We called the elders of the church to pray. We anointed with oil. We laid on hands. There were prayer vigils. There was fasting. We did everything that we could. We prayed every way we knew. Yet the dreaded disease brought about exactly the sort of physical and mental deterioration that the doctors had predicted. They suggested it would take between three and nine months. It took five. Where was God? Where was God's promise of healing? What about the promise that the prayer of faith would make the sick person well?

When cancer claims another victim, the survivors inevitably struggle with many questions about the meaning of life and death, about the sovereignty of God and about the biblical texts that seem to promise healing if we pray in faith.

A theology of healing?

When our loved ones are dying, we cry out to God for spiritual resources to meet the crisis, and God gives them. But we also cry out for physical healing here on earth, and sometimes it is denied. Where does that leave the believer who reads the Gospel accounts and gains the impression that everyone who came to Jesus for healing received it? Where are those "greater things" that Jesus said would be accomplished after he left (John 14:12)? And what about James 5:14-18 and its promise that "the prayer offered in faith will make the sick person well"? Where does one find a biblically based "theology of healing" that matches with our experience, meets our needs and challenges our faith?

We will never find such a theology of healing as long as we insist on taking a single principle or model and try to make it fit every case. The Scriptures and the experiences of life are too variegated to be squeezed into one mold or model, no matter which one is selected.

The model that says, "God always gives healing if we pray with the right sort of faith" ignores about half of the evidence of the Scriptures. The model that says, "Gifts of healing went out with the last of the apostles" ignores the irrefutable testimony of many modern believers. The model that says, "God has chosen to limit healing in this age to what medical professionals can do" makes the same error and also misunderstands the nature of a doctor's work. The model that says, "God is concerned with spiritual matters, not physical healing" is totally foreign to the principles by which Jesus lived. "God's ways are inscrutable; we cannot expect to understand" is a counsel of despair and short-circuits our responsibility to learn God's ways.

No single model is adequate. Each in its own way generates contorted biblical interpretations. Some of them also generate unnecessary and unfair loads of guilt ("You didn't pray in faith!" "Sin in your life blocked God's answer!"). Perhaps worst of all, they lead to theologies that rob the Scriptures of their challenge and handcuff God's freedom.

Because each model is inadequate on its own, we can hold to a single model only until it fails us. Then we find ourselves scrambling to find a better one. Unfortunately, we also castigate those with different models and call them unspiritual, unbiblical or unconcerned. I know whereof I speak. I have been a proponent of more than one model in my time. I have also been on the receiving end of advice from people in many camps. Simple answers are so attractive, but when they fail, who will pick up the pieces?

I do not claim to have the definitive word on healing, but I do urge that unless we find ways of holding several models in our theology at the same time, we will be unbiblical and we will be unprepared for the time when a cherished model fails. If we want to construct a well-rounded theology of healing, we would do well to begin at the critical text on prayer for healing, James 5:14-18. There are those who would urge that this text, above all others, warrants the conclusion that if we pray aright, healing will be granted. Does it really teach that?

The prayer of healing

James 5:14-18 teaches at least three things. It establishes a pattern: the sick call the elders to pray. It promises results: the sick will be healed. And it furnishes an example of how the model works: Elijah's prayers for a three-and-a-half year drought to begin and end.

Have you ever wondered about the appropriateness of the example James uses? Why Elijah? Moses and Elisha have more healings credited to them than Elijah does. If it is important to cite Elijah, why mention the drought? Why not the time he raised the widow of Zarephath's son? It would seem more relevant to James' healing context. If it is important to mention a drought, why this one? The one in Jacob's time was twice as long. If the concern is simply to find a spectacular answer to prayer, why did James not look seven verses farther back? Surely fire from heaven is more amazing than rain! All in all, it seems James has selected a very strange example to prove his point – that is, unless perhaps we have misunderstood the real significance of the example and therefore also misread the passage about healing.

Remember the time Elijah was in despair because he thought he was the only faithful man of God left? Remember how God encouraged him by telling him that there were still seven thousand faithful Israelites that he knew nothing about? What do you suppose they were doing during the three-year drought? I imagine they were praying for rain. I would have been. It would be the appropriate thing to do if the nation were perishing for lack of food and water. That is, it would be the appropriate thing if one did not know why the drought was happening and how long it would last. Seven thousand faithful believers pray for rain and nothing happens. Were they lacking faith? Were they out of step with God? No, they were simply ignorant of God's purposes and timing.

That is where Elijah was different. He knew the reason for the drought, and he knew its duration. He did not bother praying for rain until God's appointed time. When he knew the time had come, he prayed, and, not surprisingly, it rained.

Why does James cite this example? Is it to tell us that whenever we pray fervently for a drought or for rain, we can expect it to happen? Hardly. Only one out of 7,001 faithful Israelite pray-ers had that sort of success.

So, what is the lesson about praying for healing? Is it to tell us that whenever we pray fervently for physical healing, we can expect to see miracles? I think not. Does it not rather teach that if and when we have special insight into the purposes of God and the timing of God's actions, then we can speak the authoritative "Stand up and walk!" and we will see it happen? Perhaps James 5:14-18 is focused far more on discerning God's doings than on priming the pump of faith.

I have read books on healing by those who are called "faith healers." Most of them say that there are particular times when they know with certainty that God intends to heal, and they can say with confidence, "Stand up and walk!" Maybe you don't believe *any* modern faith healer can ever speak with that authority. I will join you if you believe they cannot *always* do so. Modern faith healers aside, we can hardly deny that Jesus knew what would happen when he said that. So did Peter and John in Acts 3. If we knew when and how God would heal, we could say "Stand up and walk!" with the same confidence, and it would happen. Most times it is not like that.

A balancing of models

I think it is clear that the James 5 model does not cover all cases. Are we not more often one of the seven thousand who do not know God's plans and whose prayers do not move God's hand? What then? If we insist that James 5 teaches that anyone can expect to experience a healing miracle if only their faith is adequate, then we can expect to live under a load of guilt. If we read it as I am suggesting, then it is rather a challenge to be discerning people, seeking to know God's doings and timing – a challenge to pray with confidence for a miracle when God makes intentions known, but a challenge to seek a more appropriate biblical model when God doesn't. But where do we turn for a supplementary model? We don't have far to look.

Which model would James have wanted to suppress at all costs if it had really been his concern to teach that physical healing in response to prayer was the norm, or even that knowing God's purposes and timing was the norm? Obviously the example of Job. It simply does not fit the model. Job did not know why his disease was there. He did not know if or when his health would be restored. Moreover, the purposes of God in Job's case could be fulfilled only *because* Job did not know them. *Ignorance* of God's doings was as central to God's purpose for Job as *knowledge* of God's doings was for Elijah.

But James does not suppress the example of Job. On the contrary, he holds it up high, *right in the middle of James 5*! Why? Because James never intended his readers to think that one model covers all cases. James knew that the Job model was also valid. It tells Christians something important about how God uses illness for divine purposes and how and when God brings it to an end. And it gives believers another valid model for appropriate behavior in time of sickness. The Elijah model urges "effectual fervent prayer" when we understand what God is doing. The Job model urges "perseverance" when we do not (5:11).

We cannot twist any single model and make it fit every case. A mighty miracle in response to prayer clearly brings honor to God. But so do believers who persevere without knowing why or how long they must suffer. The Job model puts its focus on "what the Lord *finally* brought about." That is why perseverance was so important. Job lived to experience not only physical healing but a doubling of his fortunes. In the end, God's character was vindicated, and Job experienced God as "full of compassion and mercy" (5:11).

But what if neither the Elijah model nor the Job model fits? Not all live to experience God's merciful healing. Some die. We simply cannot count on either God's miraculous healing (the Elijah model) or God's eventual doubling of our fortunes (the Job model). God's character is always vindicated in the end, but sometimes that end lies beyond the grave. Sometimes God expresses compassion and mercy by taking a child home, where sickness and pain are no more. When that happens, we realize that our "theology of healing" is incomplete without a third model, one which promises healing only in the life beyond.

James knew of this third model; he alluded to it in 1:12 and 4:14. So did the man who penned the seventy-third Psalm. He wrote of his struggle to find and accept this third model. It did not come easily. It troubled him when the wicked seemed to get a better deal in this life than the righteous – better health, greater wealth, fewer troubles. "When I tried to understand all this, it was oppressive to me till I entered the sanctuary of God; then I understood their final destiny" (73:16,17). The psalmist learned that God is indeed good to the pure in heart (73:1) but that the measure of that goodness is not in health or wealth or happiness. "It is good to be near God" (73:28). The good news is that God is good when a prayer of faith raises the sick (the Elijah model), when we suffer, knowing neither why nor how long (the

Job model) and even when suffering ushers us into glory (the psalmist model). "I am always with you," says the psalmist (73:23), "and being with you, I desire nothing on earth" (73:25).

James promises that "the prayer of a righteous man is powerful and effective" (5:16). It is indeed. Sometimes its effect is to change our *circumstances*, and a sick person is dramatically healed (the Elijah model). Sometimes its effect is to change our *character*, and we learn to persevere and trust the sovereignty of God (the Job model). Sometimes its effect is to change our priorities, and we rest in the assurance that "my flesh and my heart may fail but God is the strength of my heart and my portion forever" (Ps. 73:26, the psalmist model).

We dare not build our theologies, our ministries or our lives on less than these. In some cases, the authoritative "Stand up and walk!" announces the miracle that God is bringing about. In some cases, long and patient suffering is crowned with restoration and blessing. In some cases, the flesh fails and mortality is swallowed up by life (2 Cor. 5:4).

Many oversimplified and inadequate theologies of healing plague the Christian church. Almost all of them can be derived by selecting too few models. Pick any one or two of those suggested and spin out the implications. You will see what I mean. When we set aside one valid biblical model in favor of another, we find ourselves twisting the biblical texts and our experiences out of shape to make them fit, or else we find ourselves burdened with guilt about the inadequacy of our faith.

What is needed is a theology that acknowledges all three models. Together they cover all cases. The only problem is that we do not always know in advance which model fits which case. And therein lies the challenge of the Scriptures. The challenge is not one-dimensional but three, for we are called continually to discern God's ways, to persevere when we walk in the dark, and to fix our eyes on things above, not on things on earth. In all this, God never fails us. If we draw near to God, God draws near to us, and therein we experience the good life that the writer of Psalm 73 discovered.